We'd love your thoughts . . .

Your reactions, criticisms, things you did or didn't like about this Storey book. Please use space below (or write a letter if you'd prefer — even send photos!) telling how you've made use of the information . . . how you've put it to work . . . the more details the better! Thanks in advance for your help in building our library of good Storey books.

Book Title: _____

Purchased From: _____

Comments: _____

Pamela B. Art
President, Storey Publishing

_____

_____

_____

_____

Your Name: _____
(Please Print)

Mailing Address: _____

E-mail Address: _____

☐ You have my permission to quote from my comments and use these quotations in ads, brochures,
   mail, and other promotions used to market Storey books.

To order this book or any Storey title CALL 800-441-5700 or visit our website at www.storey.com

Signed _____ Date _____

Storey

e-mail: feedback@storey.com | website: www.storey.com | Printed in China | 2/07

From: ______________________________

____

____

NO POSTAGE
NECESSARY
IF MAILED
IN THE
UNITED STATES

BUSINESS REPLY MAIL

FIRST-CLASS MAIL PERMIT NO. 10 N. ADAMS MA

POSTAGE WILL BE PAID BY ADDRESSEE

STOREY PUBLISHING
PO Box 206
North Adams MA 01247-9919

STONE PRIMER

Ideas and Techniques for Incorporating
Stone In and Around Your Home

STONE
PRIMER

CHARLES McRAVEN

 Storey Publishing

The mission of Storey Publishing is to serve our customers by publishing practical information that encourages personal independence in harmony with the environment.

Edited by Deborah Balmuth, Carleen Madigan Perkins, and Nancy J. Ondra

Art direction, text design, and production by Vicky Vaughn Design

Cover design by Rob Johnson

Rock Star profiles written by Marta Alexandra Rainer

Front cover photography by © Marion Brenner: top; © Scott Calhoun: bottom left; © Jerry Pavia: bottom right; © Roger Wade: bottom center

Back cover photography for paperback edition by Karen Bussolini: middle; © Jeff Greenough: top left, bottom left and right; © Shutterstock: spine; © Roger Wade: top right

Back cover photography for hardcover edition by Karen Bussolini: middle; © Catriona Tudor Erler: bottom right; © Jeff Greenough: top left, bottom left, author's photo; © Shutterstock: spine; © Roger Wade: top right

Interior photography credits appear on page 271

Illustrations by Michael Gellatly

Indexed by Susan Olason, Indexes & Knowledge Maps

Text © 2007 by Charles McRaven

Pictured on page 5: Fireplace by Charles McRaven

Pictured on page 6: Veneer arch at the McRaven house, Free Union, Virginia.

Printed in China by Dai Nippon Printing
10 9 8 7 6 5 4 3 2 1

Library of Congress Cataloging-in-Publication Data

McRaven, Charles.
    Stone primer / by Charles McRaven.
        p. cm.
    Includes index.
    ISBN 978-1-58017-670-5 (pbk. : alk. paper)
    ISBN 978-1-58017-669-9 (hardcover jacketed : alk. paper)
    1. Stonemasonry. I. Title.
TH5401.M343 2007
693'.1—dc22
                                2007012965

CONTENTS

The Mystique of Stone

Stone is the ultimate material. It outlasts any other substance in structure, in ornamentation, in beauty. Stone, along with plants and water, is one of the few original elements of our environment. It formed our earliest tools, and it yielded the ores for our metals as we became more adept at handling those tools. Stone has always provided the material for building civilization and culture.

There exists a rare relationship between the mason and his stone, an almost mystical connection beyond labor, calluses, sweat, and skill. In the challenge of working stone, there grows a reverence for this material that makes up our planet. Its very durability, inertia, and defiance bring out the desire for mastery within the mason. Whether an Inca pounding the white granite of Machu Picchu with a harder hammerstone or a modern craftsman shaping with a diamond chip–embedded cutting wheel, the stone and the mason are the same. There is incredible pride among masons, a pride that drives us to stretch our skills, to reach beyond, to push farther.

Stone is timeless. That it might require an ancient Mycenaean mason a month or a year to shape a lintel stone was not cause for alarm; multiply him by a thousand, and the work, in evidence still today, went quickly. Spanish records tell us the mighty fortress Sacsayhuaman, above Cuzco, Peru, took 20,000 masons 50 years to build. Its 300-ton limestone outer wall stones were too big for the conquistadors to destroy.

The dedication of the mason to his stonework reaches a plane far

The fitted outer perimeter fortress stones of Sacsayhuaman, above Cuzco, Peru, also act as a retaining wall for the slope above.

above instant gratification; his work belongs to the millennia. We stand in awe of the Cyclopean stones in ancient walls, unable to grasp the scale, the demand, the sheer impossibility that primitive masons could have achieved this. Most of us are clearly outside that oneness with the stone that master masons have; it is what drives them to such perfect work.

Stoneworkers have always competed and challenged each other to achieve. In a Machu Picchu temple, one huge block of stone has with settling separated from its mortarless, zero-tolerance fit with its neighbor. The odd joint angle is not only perfectly matched, but the two inside mating surfaces, which would never be seen, are flawlessly convex and concave. I recall another stone there with 14 joint surfaces matching surrounding ones. Was such perfection mere showing off? Was it the result of religious fervor? Whatever brought it about, the craft is truly art.

An ancient civilization leaves only its stones, and perhaps a few artifacts in ceramics and rarely, in metal, to tell of its customs, its people, and its beliefs. But only the stone tells of the commitment in time, skill, and labor, and of a dedication hard to comprehend today. Didn't those old masons have anything better to do than beat on rocks month after month, year upon year? Where was the quality of their lives? The answer, or part of it, comes from master masons today, so drawn to their work that all other pursuits become ancillary. A committed mason simply wants to be laying stone.

As with any practical craft, long practice born of necessity leads to a desire for excellence. This excellence is found throughout the world. On the islands of Greece, one can find 3,000-year-old tumbled stone walls of rubble that hold back the soil or pen the sheep. Travel to Delphi and find the finely cut, almost tessellated wall of the Temple of Apollo.

Throughout Peru are countless miles of remote terraces, as finely done as those at the most famous sites of Ollantaytambo and Pisac. Peruvian rough-stone farmhouses date back to prehistory, as do flawlessly cut granite temples and watercourses and pools and steps, set without mortar and worked without steel, from long before the Inca. The elaborate water channels of finely cut blocks, directing mountain springs to terraces, homes, and ceremonial fountains, are studies in art and ingenuity. Even the steps — one-block risers or pieced treads, or flights cut from single expanses of bedrock — are studies in physics, geology, and sculpture.

Meticulously worked white granite was fitted to and cut into a natural bedrock grotto to create a ceremonial room called the Royal Tomb at Machu Picchu, Peru.

ALL MY LIFE I'D HEARD OF THE FABLED INCA stonework; Machu Picchu was always held up as the magical, hidden city where the ancients had mysteriously shaped giant boulders into perfectly fitted blocks weighing up to 70 tons. These boulders had somehow been transported great distances up mountains to promontories where they were further cut and fitted to other angled, mortised stones. So precise was the work, it defied explanation, I'd been told. Did giants do this? Aliens? A forgotten race of master engineers? Surely diminutive tribesmen who did not possess even the wheel could never have achieved such an impossibility.

I resolved to visit that country someday and see that stronghold so hidden the conquistadors never found and destroyed it. Meanwhile, though, I was learning the craft of stonework from my first stone house project as a teenager in 1948. Many years passed, many wild theories abounded. Some suggested those Peruvian stones were actually of a mysterious mortar, cast in forms to look like granite; others claimed gravity-suspending devices had been in use, their

nature now lost; maybe the super-tools used had all corroded away and no record of them survived. After all, these people had no alphabet and no written language with which to pass on their skills and knowledge, the secrets of their crafts.

When I was finally able to visit Peru in 2003 with my wife, Linda, and daughter, Amanda, it was with so many conjectural pictures in my head that I felt I could never be surprised. I was prepared for whatever evidence of the supernatural nearly seven decades of fantasy could present to me. What I found in Machu Picchu and all the other magnificent ruins in that region was very, very fine stonework, evidence of ingenuity, a dedication to the craft, and a kinship with vanished artisans who were passionate about working stone. Even the most jaded observer could not fail to be overwhelmed by the best of this work, considered the finest the world has ever known.

To me, a stonemason, it was clear how the Inca and those before them had quarried, transported, fitted, and set these stones. No magic intruded on the skilled practice of

This family photo — with my wife, Linda, and our stonemason daughter, Amanda — shows the immense scale of the stones at Sacsayhuaman. Notice the replacement fill stones at the upper left.

these masons. They used common sense, as masons always have, plus a devotion to the work and the most necessary element of all: time.

Machu Picchu, like all the fortified cities, was situated where there was an abundance of stone uphill from the site. The smaller stones could have been brought from anywhere; the larger ones inevitably came downhill from the quarries higher up the mountains. The flattened expanses within the city must have yielded many thousands of stones of all sizes. Since nearly all the huge stone blocks form retaining walls or foundations, filling behind the initial courses created level or down-sloped ground to ease the transport of stones for each next course. Retaining walls are built in this way today; we lay a course, fill behind it, then lay another, raked or battered back or deepened into the slope to hold the soil.

And how did they place those stones that are high in walls, the lintel stones that span the gateways and doorways? It was a simple matter to fill with earth to the height necessary to set the stones, then remove the earth. Hiram Bingham, Machu Picchu's discoverer, theorized this in 1911. This took time, of course, and a lot of labor, but what did a few days or months or years matter to stone that would stand for millennia?

The incredibly precise fitting of those multiton blocks, with their stepped, mortised, and angled planes, has given rise to boundless theories that involve lifting the stones to scribe exact fits or raising and lowering them multiple times for fine-tuning. Masons know, however, that it is infinitely easier to rock a stone, even a gigantic one, back onto fill for fine shaping and then rock it back into position again than it is to lift it. Knobs and sockets left on many such stones show where ropes and pry poles were used, not to lift, but

to tip these stones. And with hundreds (or perhaps thousands) of masons available, more help was on-site when needed.

Now, we do know some very large stones were moved great distances. From evidence, the method was many grass ropes pulled by many, many people. Stonemasons are good at working out ways to get difficult things done — they have to be. Most people just don't think in those terms today. We can envision droves of slaves straining to pull blocks up ramps onto the pyramids of Egypt, but even that is a stretch. The Inca did not practice slavery. A system of taxation by labor brought these workers to the building sites, eager to outdo their peers and to leave their marks for history.

Ultimately, the answer to the conundrum of the giant stones lies in the almost spiritual relationship between the mason and his stone. He devoted his life to working it, with a focus similar to religion. Each stone was a part of his life, and no matter how many times it had to be rocked, pounded, cut, repositioned, and done over again, nothing was more important. Nothing.

Typical photos of the many-acre mountaintop city of Machu Picchu such as this one show only a tiny portion (maybe 20 percent) of the actual stonework.

A modern mason, in this age of manufactured housing, decoration, and structure, has fewer opportunities to reach this oneness with his stone. Not many of us will dedicate so much time, effort, and concentration to the job of placing stones. And even for those so committed, the builder, owner, or patron who will spend the kind of money required for such work is rare indeed.

Essentially, stonework comes down to what the mason is trying to achieve. What artistic statement does his beehive shelter, his moongate, or his waterfall make? We're out of the realm of pure function here; an ugly wall can hold sheep in, but that same wall can be, and often is, flowing and rhythmic and timeless and beautiful. The Wave Organ that Tomas Lipps and George Gonzalez built in San Francisco is experiential art; people are emotionally moved by the masterful work of the masons' hands and eyes and hearts. That is its function, albeit one more complex than penning sheep. It's all about the mason's desire to reach farther, create finer, come closer to the ultimate potential that is in the stone.

I've often likened laying a single stone to a move in a chess game: it changes all the options that follow. And while laying stone can be planned, outlined, and even diagrammed ahead of time, the best work seldom is. An innate feel for what is right grows in the mason, as it does in any artist. Just as a painting can be reduced to a formula, but the formula may not reproduce the painting, so it is with a section of stonework. There is a feel, a flow, a nonregimentation to good stonework that either is there or it isn't. Often, the mason himself cannot tell how he achieved it.

Basalt columns combine with closely fitted stone walls, metal sculptures, and a waterfall in this public "pocket park" in Bend, Oregon.

The landscape architect Robert Murase once planned a placement of basalt columns for water to course over and through for the Microsoft Corporation campus in Seattle. These columns are formed naturally, in hexagonal lengths reminiscent of some quartz crystal formations. Murase had designed the feature carefully for the effect he wanted to achieve. But when the crane had stacked the stone columns from shipping, their random placement suddenly struck the architect as the ideal composition. With only minor adjustments, he was able to direct the flow of water not as he'd envisioned it, but for a more artistic effect. This knowing and recognizing what feels right is part of the essence of good stonework.

The Wave Organ, creation of master masons George Gonzalez and Tomas Lipps, in San Francisco. The sound of the waves is carried through pipes to listening posts on the long jetty. The carved stone came from a public architectural salvage yard.

Stonework continues to fascinate. Its appeal transcends nationality, race, and educational background. A suburban housewife and a back-country hillside farmer can want stone for vastly different purposes, in an equally vague but compelling way. A walled terrace for both of them may hold precious crop soil or a flower bed, or a necessary path or steps, but it also proclaims beauty and permanence, and a willingness for the builders to put more of themselves into their surroundings. If either of them had used railroad ties or concrete blocks or brick, the message to the rest of us would have been so different.

You will eventually develop your own philosophy of stonework. It will no doubt include something of the work involved, the durability, the *rightness* of stone used properly. Once past the initial frustrations of time involved, the resistance of the substance to your shaping, and the sore muscles, you can reach a higher level of appreciation of the craft and the art.

My hope is that you will.

Charles R. McRaven

PART 1

Starting with Stone

Massive, permanent, and stunning, good stonework adds character to the home landscape. Though it might look difficult, such work is entirely within reach of the average homeowner. With a little direction and a patient frame of mind, any active person can turn a pile of stone into a work of art.

My crew and I built this drystone wall at a spectacular mountaintop site near the Blue Ridge in Virginia. The ledge sandstone varies in color and texture so each stone's character stands forth.

I f you are drawn to stonework, your subconscious will form images of what you want yours to look like. Central to this envisioning is a little knowledge

The Right Stone for the Right Project

of the stone types. There is so much variety: deeply pocked and weathered granite, top-of-the-ground limestone, freshly cut rainbow sandstone, massive basalt blocks, fieldstone with lichens and moss, shales, quartzes, gneisses, and black volcanic stone.

Stone comes in all shapes, sizes, colors, weights, and textures. A wall of dark basalt, for instance, is going to absorb light and reveal little detail in the stone surfaces. Even the joints may recede visually in low light. By contrast, pale sandstone will reflect light. Either of these virtual opposites can blur into an amorphous mass if all the stones are the same shade.

LEFT: The door in this mortared stone retaining wall leads to an underground storage room.

A large stone anchors the wall and draws the eye to its lichened surface.

Cutting into weathered sandstone reveals color and grain to accent a drystone wall. This work was done by beginning stonemason Grant Connette under my supervision.

Mixing stone types is sometimes effective, but it can also result in a circus of shades, colors, and textures that won't work. It's better to stick with one type, varying the shapes, sizes, and shades so individual stones stand out but the whole is attractive and fits with any natural stone of the region.

Often we are asked to build with a specific type of stone the owner may have chosen from a stoneyard. Just as often, that stone isn't compatible with the natural stone along nearby roadsides or in the woods; it may not even be right for the project. For instance, precisely cut ashlar, with its tight geometric joints, isn't right for a meandering stream or waterfall, just as round, glacial granite boulders aren't right in Tennessee ledge limestone country. Using indigenous stone is the first step toward getting the right look; doing the work well is the rest of the requirement.

The characteristics of stone have a lot to do with how it was used by the old masons, but even when masons had only harder stones as tools, intricate shaping evolved. While rough work in retaining walls and simple houses was usually the norm, really fine examples of stonework exist in temples, houses, and public buildings that wanted to show what could be achieved, regardless of the stone's workability.

Common Types of Stone

Sandstone and limestone were, and still are, the easiest stones to cut and shape. There are several kinds of each. Igneous rocks such as granite and basalt are much harder to work, but they have their uses, too.

Sandstone

Sandstone can be coarse and crumbly, fine-grained and hard, or anything between these contrasts. It's a sedimentary rock that was laid down in strata (layers) in prehistoric lake beds and seas. The layers give it a horizontal grain. Weathering breaks off exposed strata into blocks. These blocks weather more, age, and soften at the edges, becoming what we call fieldstone (as opposed to freshly quarried stone). For many years, I worked only with field sandstone because that was abundant in my native Arkansas. I like the look of age, the patina, and the lichen on the faces. I delight in building a new wall that look as if it's been there for generations.

Actually, it doesn't take long for quarried sandstone to develop a softer look, because the cut faces weather relatively quickly. Dan Smith, a master mason I worked with on our house in the 1980s, mixed cut faces, which he liked, with weathered fieldstone on our arched porch foundation. Today, only a mason can detect which is which

In a structural situation, such as a tall chimney or a supporting column, it's best to stay away from the soft, crumbly kind of sandstone. But in fact, it can be as soft as the mortar used, since mortar normally is the weak link in the stonework. In such a place where strength and crush-resistance are important, you can always overbuild — a 4-foot-thick column holds up more than a 2-foot-thick one.

The harder sandstone, commonly called quartzite by masons, tends to have more strength and cuts cleaner. It is gratifying to shape a piece of dense sandstone, having it split crisply under your chisel like an apple (well, maybe not *that* easily). It doesn't pit or weather as fast as the softer stone but it will age nicely in time, even supporting the growth of lichens eventually, if in a moist location. Real quartzite is metamorphic, almost white in color, and has no easily worked grain.

Sandstone comes in almost all colors. I've seen it red, yellow, orange, brown, gray, bluish, and sometimes in rainbows, when freshly cut. These colors usually fade in time, to a gray, brown, or reddish, depending on the sand color in the stone. For years I avoided a chocolate-purple sandstone that's plentiful up the slopes of the Appalachian Mountains west of the Shenandoah Valley because I didn't like the color. When weathered or lichened, it looked all right, so I'd mix in an occasional stone for variety,

GOING NATIVE

SANDSTONE IS A PLEASURE to work with, but don't select it just because of that characteristic. If sandstone isn't native to your region, it's going to look out of place. If you have limestone instead, for instance, using that will blend better with the surroundings. If you're in granite or greenstone or basalt country, I'd say go with what's native. This could mean a lot more work, however, depending on how usable the native stone is.

For example, we built a fireplace and chimney in Fauquier County, Virginia, using the local greenstone, which had veins of quartz in it. Somehow, in more than 50 years of masonry, I had never used this particular stone. I supposed it to be as workable as the quarried greenstone a few counties south, near my home. Not so! This stuff broke chisels. It refused to be scored with diamond-chip cutting blades. The stone melted like lava under the heat of the blades, solidifying again after the attempted cut. Blades wore out quickly. We went through hundreds of tons of that stone to get the relatively few we needed. It was good-looking rock, but mean.

Perhaps your native rock will be easier to work with, but even if it isn't, you'll know it was worth the effort when you see the end result. It will just look *right*.

whether in a wall or as flagstone. I could find it everywhere, usually already in layers, but I just didn't like the color. Then I noticed that weathering muted it rather quickly, since the stone is relatively soft. I also noticed that this color worked well when mixed in with other stones that might be too gray, or too tan, or even too white. The whole wall aspect changed for the better, toned down, when the chocolate-colored rock was added to the mix. I use it more now, and no one else seems to notice or complain. One customer liked it so much she had us use it everywhere: chimney, house walls, pathways, and retaining walls. It's simply a matter of taste.

Limestone

Limestone, about as workable as sandstone and denser in grain, is still widely used. Another sedimentary rock, it was long the material of choice in the United States for business buildings, as an alternative to brick. It was usually square or rectangle-cut, with protruding dressed faces. Today, its use in commercial buildings has, sadly, been replaced with concrete blocks.

Limestone can come in a range of colors, as well as many shades of gray. I once worked with a bluish stone along the Kentucky River that got its color from blue clay among the layers. Generally, limestone is an uninspiring gray I associate with tombstones, but aged, corroded-surface limestone is beautiful, particularly with lichens and pocked faces.

Dry Stone Conservancy members restored this limestone driveway entry, complete with traditional upright capstones.

Because it is sedimentary, limestone sometimes is useful as flagstone material. We laid a floor of 2-inch-thick limestone slabs in our log cabin in Missouri in the 1970s. These came directly from along the creek next to the site. We didn't cut any of it — just laid it in random shapes. And because it had been tumbled by the water, it needed no further smoothing. Two coats of masonry sealer followed by periodic waxing made a low-upkeep floor.

My friend Scot Land built an imposing house in Seattle with a tower, exterior walls, and retaining walls of cut limestone. A vein of brown relieved the gray color and we found some other brown stones to mix in, picking up that warmth. The result was a pleasing structure that drew a sense of strength from the stone.

Like sandstone, limestone is relatively easy to work. Both types of stone tend to occur in layers. This means that many of the stones naturally have the flat tops and bottoms necessary for good stone structure. The faces may be left natural, partially shaped, or further dressed for the disciplined look of ashlar, that all-straight-line cut stone. Of course, not every stone is easily usable as found, but with cutting, these rocks have great potential.

Granite

Granite is the third common stone we see in most stonework. It is igneous, harder and stronger than either sandstone or limestone, and in some ways preferable. Its generally rough composition leaves a more porous surface to which lichens easily adhere. Aged granite corners round pleasantly, and the surfaces bleach in the sun.

Fresh-cut granite can be gray, blue, green, red, or brown. A hard stone, it polishes well and is used this way for commercial buildings, interiors, countertops, and tombstones. The quartz in granite gives it a sparkle and depth when polished.

I like granite fieldstone with its patina. I try to keep cut surfaces at the joints or backs of the stones, so that only the aged surfaces show. Part of this is aesthetic; the rest is practical, since the stone is not easy to work. Carbide-tipped tools and diamond-chip blades make the job less difficult.

Stonemason Kevin Fife restored this granite wall at the Old Meeting House Cemetery in Danville, New Hampshire.

Basalt

Another common stone is basalt, which is formed much like granite but without the granular makeup. Usually black or dark gray, this hard, dense igneous rock requires about the same tenacity to shape as granite. It can be used for most stonework, but is more difficult to shape, since it has no grain. Basalt is generally found in the western and northwestern parts of the United States.

As with all other stones, usable chunks of basalt can be found as fieldstone. This simply means more hunting for the right rock, instead of shaping it. Many masons prefer this approach anyway, for a rugged, more natural look to their work.

Other Types of Stone

Shales, slates, aggregates, lava, greenstone, and other, more obscure types of stone can be used in masonry, but they usually are less appealing and more hassle. At a commercial stoneyard, you will be confronted with a bewildering choice of stones, with confusing names meant to enhance their salability. A cherrystone or a bluestone or a weatherface or a Shenandoah might have the look you either want or don't want, but the names give no hint of what the rock is or how it'll behave. Sometimes the stoneyard staff can give you this information, and sometimes they can't. Prepare yourself with a basic knowledge of stone and its various characteristics so you can choose the right material for your project.

Of course, any stonemason will tell you that learning about stone isn't something you can do only from a book. Most of us learned how to work and apply stone types by experimenting or by working with other masons who had learned. A mason who found that soft sandstone couldn't support a house foundation would avoid it in the future. If another mason told us blue mountain granite broke his chisels but looked good when laid, we would figure that into our proposed uses of the stone. But don't let inexperience stop you from learning about stone; if you're just getting into working with stone, you can still get good results if you do your homework *before* deciding on the kind of stone you want.

There is a world of technical information about stones: geological names, structural data, and all kinds of minutiae. As a mason, your primary concern will be what the stone looks like, whether it is aged or freshly cut, and its workability and potential. You will need to adapt to each stone type's characteristics to get the result you want.

Some types of rock, like this greenstone, have no discernible grain, which makes it difficult to shape.

GO WITH THE GRAIN

ANY OF THESE STONES — limestone, sandstones, granite — can be rough-shaped with a stone maul (a blunt-edged, heavy hammer) or cut with hammer and chisel, given enough time and effort. Reading the grain in the stone is a necessity for splitting it, which is a good first step in shaping. Often cutting across the grain can be helped along by scoring with a masonry blade on a grinder or circular saw; then the stone can be broken the rest of the way with chisel or maul. I limit this scoring to surfaces that won't be seen, or grind away the smooth-cut evidence.

Edwin Hamilton PETALUMA, CA

ABOVE: Edwin Hamilton created this tightly fitted stone wall for the Library Terrace Garden at the San Francisco Botanical Garden at Strybing Arboretum.

OPPOSITE: A freestanding mortared wall accents and protects this mature tree on a client's property.

Edwin Hamilton stepped inside York Minster, one of England's finest cathedrals, and immediately understood why his two mentors (one of whom was Tomas Lipps, of the Stone Foundation) back in Marin County, California, had advised him to come to Europe. "You have no idea how strong the resonance and power of stone craft is until you go see these masterworks for yourself," they told him.

Edwin bought a one-way ticket. After two years he had hitchhiked and labored his way through England, Scotland, France, Italy, North Africa, and beyond, building stone houses and bridges. "It's the same today as in the days of cathedral building," he says. "Masons are nomadic." After two decades, he says he'd still go anywhere for the right project.

Edwin's formidable rites of passage of apprenticeships and travel, which eventually included three "humbling" months exploring the ruins of Peru, shaped his personal aesthetic as stonemason and sculptor. "I have an eye toward the monumental," he says.

This quality of grandeur was first realized in an installation of four granite water vessels at the Queens County Civic Courthouse in New York, a project designed and commissioned by public artist Anna Valentina Murch. It took Edwin eight months just to prepare for this task, from buying a 1944 forklift big enough to haul 27 tons of

granite, to designing and fabricating the sawing equipment, to hunting down a shop space big enough to accommodate the materials (he still works in it). It then took him a year of daily labor to craft the basins.

Edwin calls this the first of two landmark projects in his professional life. The second, a ski lodge in Idaho designed by the renowned architect Thierry Despont, gave him the opportunity to create, among other things, a 42-foot front elevation of sandstone: the architect took "a leap of faith," Edwin says, in his skill. In tackling the challenge of how to move huge stones 35 feet in the air, Edwin says he was finally able "to think on similar lines as cathedral builders."

A job he recently completed on a coastal California estate was unique in that it utilized exclusively stone indigenous to the site — in all forms, down to the crushed rock used as seeded aggregate in the concrete driveway and even the sand by-product of the crushing process, which was used for mortar to build a stone wall

I have an eye toward the monumental.

(pictured above). That wall wends its way gracefully over a grade change and around a "beautiful tree with a desire for lawn; it just about designed itself," he says.

The thread running through his many works, both architectural and sculptural, is his promise of intention, a concept he carries from his early days of apprenticeship when he learned to place each stone "with the intention of it being there for 500 years . . . and more." If you take the time and do it right, he says, "a dialogue happens between the mason and each stone." He attributes this fundamental dialogue as the link between his sculpturally influenced work and even the most traditional masonry. The satisfaction of discovering each new stone's intention remains the same, be the work carving enormous granite masses for a public plaza or creating a small drystone wall in the woods behind a house.

"Even the most rudimentary stone wall embodies all the principles of good masonry," he says, "and it's just incredibly beautiful if it's built right."

Finding the Right Stone

One of the things I have to contend with is the general perception of stone quality — or the lack of it — for building. Too many times, people who want stonework done will assure me they have lots of rocks on the place. They want me to use these, both to save money and because they're there, a matching part of the place already. Unfortunately, nearly all of the stone lying around houses has been picked over; what's left are the rejects or the stones weren't suitable in the first place. On average, you'll sort through probably 100 of these rocks to find just one that is easily usable.

Purchasing from Stoneyards

Purchasing stone at a stoneyard isn't necessarily an easy solution to this problem. There, you must buy by the ton or the pallet, and you're seldom allowed to pick and choose, because what you would leave would likely go unsold. Follow the basic rule that stone in any structure should stay in place without mortar. This means selecting stones with flat tops and bottoms, regardless of their other characteristics. Unfortunately, a lot of stone offered by stoneyards doesn't meet this criterion, since they tend to cater to masons who glue their stones in place with mortar.

If too much of your project is built with stoneyard stone, you will end up with a good percentage of stone not usable for building. You still may be able to use those rejects in a rock garden or for edging flower beds, so they won't be a total loss, but over the course of the building project, you'll end up spending a lot of money for those "decorative" stones.

That's why independent sojourns into natural sources of stone are so valuable. While they might seem time-consuming or expensive, these jaunts offer you a unique opportunity to choose every rock and to have each rock fit into your scheme. That makes the trips more, not less, cost-effective. I like to have a supply of hand-gathered stone to mix in with commercially gathered pallets I buy. Mixing the stones makes for a more interesting wall.

So, where do you find good rocks? Look in lots of places besides stoneyards: in the woods, along roadsides, and in farmers'

FIELDSTONE VERSUS QUARRIED STONE

REGARDLESS OF WHAT STONE TYPE you choose, avoid any stones that have cracks or faults, because these will come apart if you have to shape them. And if the stone you need has to support something heavy, or span a space, don't use fieldstone unless it's sound. With just about any stone that's exposed to the weather for long periods, as is fieldstone, water gets into minute cracks and freezes; eventually these cracks enlarge and lengthen. In time, the stones will separate into smaller stones (called mechanical breakdown) and, a long time later, into sand. (That is, of course, how we get sand, and eventually soil, when organic matter is thrown into the mix.)

You get a good picture of what's going on with weathering stone when you cut into it with a chisel. The surface sort of crumbles, even if it's hard granite, before you get down to the dense, stronger stone underneath. Freshly quarried stone is almost always stronger, even if it's bright. It'll age, in time.

Pallets of good field sandstone can be found at a local stoneyard. These long stones are much more usable than short, blocky ones.

IF YOU GO SEARCHING FOR ROCKS on public land, make sure you know the difference between national forests and national parks. The U.S. Forest Service, which allows stone collecting, is under the jurisdiction of the Department of Agriculture, while national parks are under the Department of the Interior. Different philosophies. Forest ranger stations issue stone-gathering permits for set fees, allowing you to gather a specific quantity of stone for personal use from specified areas in a certain period of time and number of trips. In return, you must follow the rules, including prohibitions against using machinery or vehicles off roads, gathering from streambeds, and gathering for commercial use or resale.

fields (but be sure to get permission first). Another good resource is rock recycled from old chimneys, foundations, cellars, and retaining walls. You can go ahead and choose just the rocks you have a use for and leave the others. They'll continue to look scenic, and no one will know you took their neighbors.

Gathering Your Own Stone

When I need stone for my own use, I like to get a National Forest permit and go scouting. Sometimes there'll be a trout stream close, and I'll make it an all-day event. It does mean carrying each stone out of the woods, or dragging it or rolling it end over end. Sometimes I find good stone up a slope and tumble down a dozen or so at a time, in stages. Steep rock slides are dangerous, and should be avoided; it's easy to get hurt and/or buried in one.

As you gain experience, you'll be able to evaluate and gather less-than-ideal stones that you know you'll have to shape, cut, or split for use. It's easiest to choose rocks that may not be perfect as is but are close to the shape you need so you have minimal shaping to do. Seeing the desired shape in the existing stone is something that will come with practice. If you're one of those purists who want to use every rock just as they find it, you'll have to spend more time searching.

Because both limestone and sandstone occur in layers, finding some usually means more is nearby. I recall a mountaintop a friend owned in West Virginia, where rectangular sandstone was layered in a jumble almost 4 feet deep. The soil had washed away from between the rocks, leaving them ready for the taking. Every stone was usable, and in about an hour I had loaded my pickup with nearly 2 tons without moving it. This was a sea bottom once, my geologist friends tell me. Fossils abound in some of the stones.

Roadsides and field edges can also provide a wealth of usable stones. Farmers stacked stones out of their fields every year as plowing turned them up. In good rock country, such a pile can be a bonanza. After I pick through a pile, I always consolidate the rejects again, to keep the farmer happy. I've found such stone for anywhere from free to just a minimal charge for a pickup load.

My late friend Bill Cameron was a traveling mill-supply salesman during the Depression, and had plans for a stone lakeside cottage. He collected individual stones along rural roads in Missouri and Arkansas in the trunk of his car for several years, just a few at a time as he came across them. Eventually, he had enough to have the cottage built with them. I have this mental picture of him wrestling stones into his car while wearing shiny shoes, a three-piece suit, and a hat. Bill was from farm country in Northern Ireland and worked 14-hour days all his life. The point is, if you stay at it, a few at a time add up nicely.

If you know a geologist, he or she can tell you where certain types of stone exist, and you can go hunting there. That doesn't mean all the rocks will be usable, but it does get you into the right territory. If you find a concentration of stone somewhere — at the foot of a steep slope, for example — but none of it appears usable, it's probably been picked over. Dig down and you're apt to find good stones under these rejects. There is usually more than just the visible surface layer.

Keep in mind that *finding* rock isn't the same as *getting* it. My neighbor in central Virginia owns a mountainside, clear up to the top. I know there's good granite there, but only because nobody's gone up to get it; it's steep and rough, and beyond any semblance of roadway. Getting that stone down would cost a great deal more than it's worth.

Sometimes, you'll see a corner of a stone protruding from the ground, and you'll imagine a perfect rock under there. I use a big 6-foot digging bar and a 3-foot one to turn these up if I can. If they're too big to budge, they stay there. Sometimes the rest of the rock is a total waste; sometimes it isn't. That's part of the adventure of rock hunting in the wild.

Stone-collecting Pointers

Here are a few more suggestions to keep in mind as you go out to gather your own stones.

Ask first. Always get permission from landowners before collecting stone from their property.

Gabe Silver selects a stone from the remains of a pile. Projects require more stone than is actually used, so the builder can choose the right stone for the right spot.

Look for flat surfaces. A rock isn't a rock isn't a rock, when it comes to laying it in its place in your structure. I'll repeat this axiom several times: *A stone should be so shaped that it will stay in place without mortar.* That makes cementing it a no-brainer, with the mortar acting mostly as fill — a cushion to distribute the weight evenly. In general, you'll want to select stones that are flat on the top and bottom. You don't necessarily want every stone to be this way, but for the structure's sake, most of them should be; one rock sits on whatever's below, and the next one up sits on this one, lapping over the vertical joint to the one alongside. Occasional odd-shaped character stones can look good, but that predominantly horizontal joint will be necessary to hold everything together.

Seek out squares. For chimneys, piers, and square columns, you'll need lots of cornerstones. Get all you can that are square or close to it. Shaping corners is time-consuming, and visible new cuts are never as attractive as the weathered faces. In a 3-foot chimney side, you may well need two out of three stones that have good corners.

Traditionally, in both Europe and America, the best stones were used in the corners and at door and window openings in any structure. Sometimes these corner stones were set to protrude a little, or "stand proud,"

for emphasis. They are called quoins in this style of building. With a liberal use of mortar, less perfect ones were used to fill between. That's still sound practice, although we try to make all the joints as tight as is practical.

Gather more than you need. Wherever you get your stone, be sure to collect at least 50 percent more than you'll need, so you'll have choices when you build with it. Getting twice as much as you need is better, and you'll always find uses for the leftovers.

Cover your tracks. If you've dug loose a lot of soil getting subterranean stones, cover the raw earth with leaves and brush to keep it from washing. Whether on a farmer's land or in the woods, you want to leave light tracks. It's wise to maintain good relations with whoever owns the land where you're gathering stones because you may well want to come back later. Always respect the property of others. It'll help keep intact our image as honest craftsmen.

Seeing the Possibilities

No matter where you get your stone, it is necessary to visualize what you're going to do with the stones before you gather them. Some people do this in their heads; others make exact, measured drawings. Of course, the trouble with these drawings is that you won't find stones to match the exact shapes drawn or even desired. You can get close, but the rocks will be the ultimate deciding factors.

Whether you gather your own stones or buy from a stoneyard or supplier, look over the stones first. Will they stay put in your wall? You'll need stones with a flat top and bottom, and enough thickness to be stable. Round rocks are frustrating, and usually end up sort of floating in mortar. Odd-shaped chunks often defy your ability to lay them, no matter how good they look beforehand.

A stone that looks doubtful in the woods or on a stoneyard pallet won't look any better once you get it home. If you find only reject stones, don't take them. This pursuit of laying stone will be challenging enough even with near-perfect material. After you've gained experience, you might decide to shape poor stone, perhaps because you got it cheap, but that's not a good idea. You'll get frustrated easily.

You see, you might spend only a minute or two laying a well-shaped stone. But cutting a poor one to that same shape could take you half an hour, and it might shatter just as you're finishing. Unless you become proficient at cutting stone, the shaped one won't look as good as the natural one.

Be on the lookout for stones that will fit somewhere, if not in your current project. I've already mentioned corner stones — they're invaluable,

Rarely is there an unusable stone, but the one at the top will require a lot of shaping to fit most projects. The other is usable as it is, having a flat top and bottom and acceptable faces.

In a curved wall such as this stair tower, it is often necessary to use vertical stones. This is mortared veneer of 6-inch-thick stone with steel masonry ties holding the stone to the framework.

so get as many as you can. The same goes for long stones, not only for their wonderful, strong look in any wall, but also for their use as binder or anchor stones.

In time, you'll learn which stones need only a point knocked off or a jagged edge straightened, and what's involved to correct either flaw. It's a good idea to take your hammer and chisel into the woods to find out what you'll be up against if you try to work with what you've found. Even if you count your time for nothing, that time spent reclaiming bad rocks will be time you could spend doing something more productive, or more fun.

At the stoneyard, of course, you won't be allowed to bang away at rocks. Still, check over the pallets to confirm that most of the stones are usable as they are. If they're not, don't buy them. You'll pay more for good stuff, but it's worth it.

Moving Large Stones

I like big stones in any work I do. That means equipment, though, or lots of help. Experience will tell you it takes only a little longer to set a large stone than a small one and you make a lot of progress quickly if you can handle the big stuff. If not, you waste a lot of time trying. But once in place, that big rock is always cause for wonder at how you got it there.

FOUR WAYS TO MOVE STONE

IF YOU'RE WORKING ALONE, sometimes the best way to move large stones is to drag them rather than lift them. Here are a few good ways to help get stone from point A to point B.

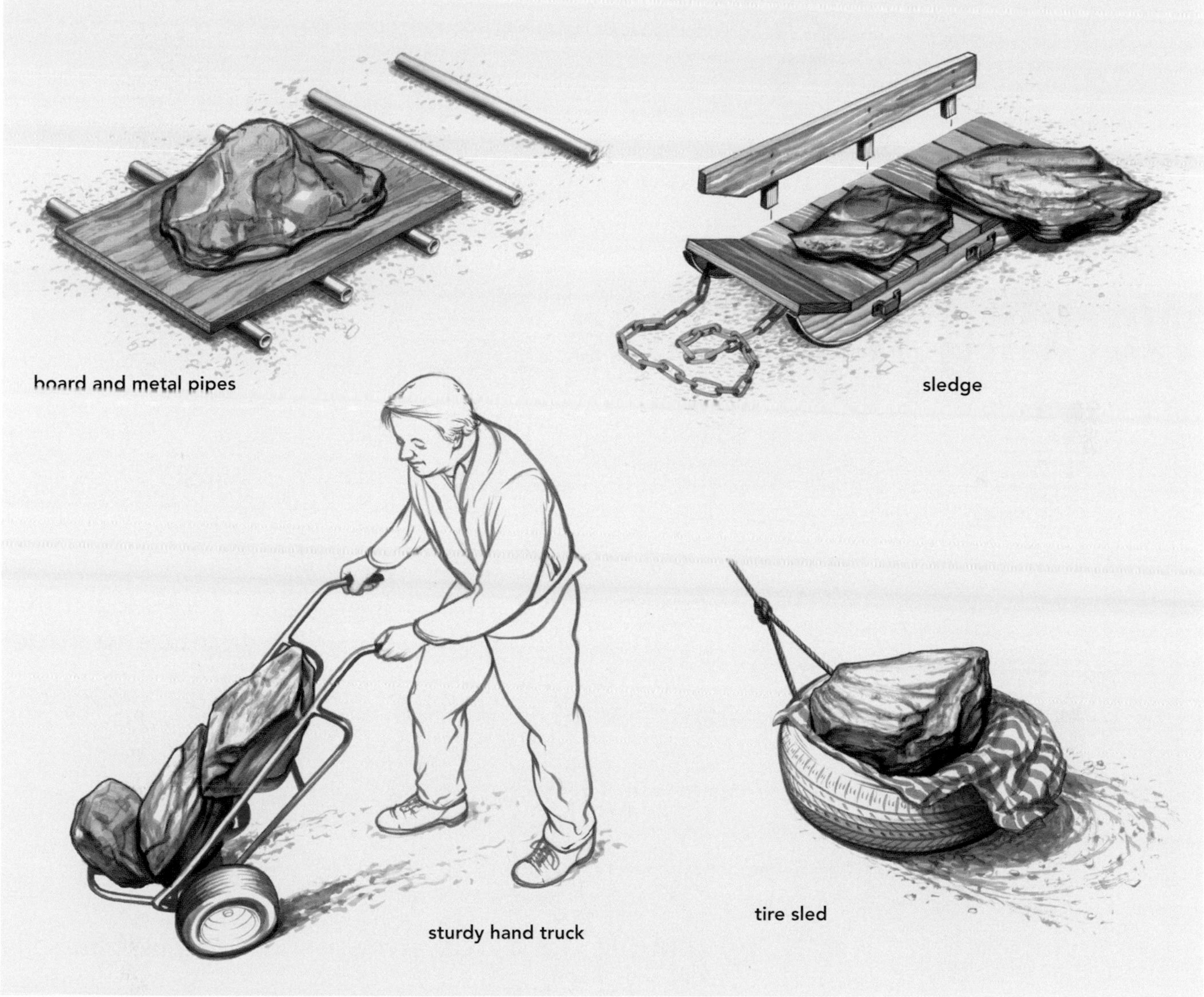

board and metal pipes
sledge
sturdy hand truck
tire sled

There is a limit to what even two reasonably able-bodied people can handle. Often, we'll pull stones up a heavy plank, or winch them out of the woods. The right rock is worth a lot of effort, if it's truly the right one. Be extra careful about safety, though; you might scrape a shin or smash a finger on a small stone, but a really big one that gets away can do real damage. Lifting slings should be soundly attached, don't stand under elevated stones, and try hard not to get your extremities caught between boulders. Big rocks don't cut you any slack. For tips on working with big stones once you get them home, see Handling Large Stones on page 78.

tone is beautiful in its natural state. But just because
a stone looks intriguing on the forest floor or in a
natural outcropping doesn't mean it's ready to be put to

Working with Stone

use in a project. Sometimes a little (or a lot of) shaping is needed to make it fit. Fortunately, a mason's skill can turn even stones with no flat sides into something structurally sound. Todd Campbell, a mason in Utah, works stone minimally (and sometimes with very primitive techniques) in order to keep it as close as possible to its natural state. By contrast, Toru Oba, a mason in Virginia, carefully shapes nearly every stone. Developing an appreciation of the unique traits of stone, and using them in a way that shows them off to advantage, is the way to make sure your stonework will be a joy to behold.

OPPOSITE: A stone hammer and a chisel are the two most basic tools needed for shaping stone.

Stone is mass, first of all. Tall, spindly columns of fieldstone just don't work, and tall, skinny chimney flues in stone aren't right, either. I recently refused to build a stone flue at the end of a restored log cabin because the owner wanted it 18 inches wide and 27 feet high. It would have looked better to use stovepipe. Another owner did let me widen a similar wood-stove flue on a cabin so that at least it looked as if a fireplace was inside.

Thin, stick-on rocks so in evidence in subdivisions look like what they are: poor imitations of real stonework. No mass here, as even an untrained eye can see; the stone is practically paper-thin.

Because stone is heavy and hard and long-lasting, and because it claims such a big place in our heritage, it must be treated right. Any structure of stone should appear massive, permanent, and maintenance-free. If it's a building, it should have the appeal of shelter and a feeling of safety. Stonework should never be flimsy or poorly done.

Minimize the Mortar

Mortar should never be more than fill, and the less that shows, the better. One of the most common mistakes new masons make is wide mortar joints, which leave the impression that stones were pushed indiscriminately into a wet concrete wall. Remembering the rule that a stone should stay in place even without mortar will remind you to keep the joints to a minimum. That rule, of course, requires more shaping, or more hunting for the right shapes,

Recessed mortar joints and tight fitting let these stones look natural, not contrived.

and that, in turn, means more time and/or labor. The temptation is strong to leave wide joints to get on with the job, but that's a big mistake; those sloppy expanses of mortar will be there for everyone to see from now on. The excess mortar will, in fact, dominate and get more notice than your stonework will.

It is true that mortar plays a more important part in applications like stone veneer, especially if it's thin. A dry-laid look will let rainwater in the cracks, to freeze and pop stones loose, if the mortar even holds at all. A substantial mortar joint is necessary, but it can be struck back so it's not obvious. Any mortar joint, when recessed, is in shadow and doesn't dominate the stone visually. Even in veneer, the

Many of the stones Toru Oba used in this dramatic freestanding fireplace extend all the way through the structure.

This is possibly the ugliest "stone-work" in existence, showing poor material, lack of skill, and no pride in workmanship.

mortar should not have a "character" of its own; in other words, it should never compete with the stone. That means no "rope" pattern (common in 20th-century American houses before 1950) or any other pattern, no color, and no texture of any kind. The mortar should not include finger- or hand prints, nor should it be sloppy, rough, or oozing.

If mortar gets on the faces of the stones, it's best to sponge it off immediately. Leaving it to be wire-brushed off later will leave a white stain. Ideally, you should lay the mortar bed for the stones so it's set back from the edge. If you lay the mortar bed out to the same face as the stone, you might be tempted to leave it there, and that's not good. You will make yourself lots of hard work wire-brushing the damp mortar back into the rock for the recessed look. The consistency of the mortar itself also plays a part. If it's too wet, it's likely to ooze; if it's too dry, it won't bond to the stone well and won't seal out rainwater. It shouldn't be at all crumbly. It is best to control the appearance and style you will see forever right from the beginning, during the construction.

Lay Stone in Layers

Because stone — particularly sedimentary stone such as sandstone and limestone — normally occurs in layers, it should be used that way. Even igneous rocks tend to be found in nature lying flat instead of standing up, so that's natural here, too. Besides the strength and bonding that horizontal stonework gives, it's also pleasing to the eye.

I recall an apprentice who'd been a carpenter, but who really wanted to be a mason. He worked for me for two years but had no aptitude for the aesthetics of stone. The last job he did for me was in my temporary absence. He stood same-size veneer stones up on an aboveground foundation wall vertically, side by side. They fit better that way, he explained

TRAINING YOUR EYE

YOU DON'T HAVE TO BE AN ARTIST to be a good mason, but it helps. Much of the reason stone is used today is its appearance, and the better it looks, the more desirable it is. Just as using a camera does not make you a photographer, simply laying rock does not make you a stonemason. You can, however, train yourself to be pretty good by learning what does and does not make a beautiful wall. Develop your eye by looking at the work of other masons to see what works well and what doesn't; this will go a long way toward improving the look of your own projects.

to the owner of the house, who made him take out most of them before I got there. I made him take out the rest. The effect on the appearance of the house, which was already up, made it look like it was balanced on playing cards on edge. This man's mistake was that he knew the concrete basement actually supported the house structurally, and it didn't matter to him how the stone went. It mattered to the owner, and it mattered very much to me. I hope he's enjoying carpentry, somewhere.

The rule of laying stone horizontally can trip you up as well. Too many stones of the same size, shape, or color are bad together, and so is an unbroken horizontal joint if it goes too far. For those reasons, you'll want to use stones of different heights and colors in each course (layer) you set, and include a variety of sizes in the general area you're working on.

If you have any "eye" at all, you'll generally see which stone should come next. Stand back often and look critically at what you've done. Do you see a blob of chocolate stones in a generally light-colored wall? Take out a few and replace them with lighter browns or grays. Are there too many small stones? Put in a big one as a visual focal point. Avoid two large stones next to each other, though; set those two nice big ones several feet apart, with smaller ones between.

Alex Rucker's tightly fitted granite driveway entry wall shows none of the mortar that binds it. His combination of different shapes and sizes shows his artistic eye.

Include a Little Variety

Do not be afraid of irregular-shaped stones if you use them sparingly. Those "interesting" stones often become focal points in a wall. In our house, we have a stone wall in the breakfast nook of our kitchen that contains a large, oddly shaped stone. When our children were little, they called it the "elephant" rock. This "reject" rock features a distinctive "trunk" and a raised section on its surface for the "ear." We love that rock.

During the Stone Foundation symposium in Virginia in 2001, the stonemasons built a serpentine wall that climbed a hill, using many arched and curved rocks. Those shapes became an important element to the success of that wall. In a straight wall, those stones would have to be used only sparingly.

How much irregularity is too much? Because this is subjective, it's hard to reduce to rules. In my experience, if you put the wrong stone in, it'll nag at you until you take it out. If you refuse to do so, that section of wall will never look right, to you or to others. Now, that stone might be ideal for another spot, depending on its peculiarities. It just doesn't go in this spot, so take it out. Tweaking your work is worth it in the long term. You'll never regret it.

This wall was the result of a Stone Foundation competition among teams of masons. This winning section was done by Kevin Fife's team, and shows good use of tie-stones, capstones, ledge pattern, and varied stone sizes.

As the look of stonework is subjective, it offers a lot of latitude. That's why all stone walls are different, even those done by the same mason using similar stone. The stone itself has something to say about how it's laid, even if that influence is subtle. Only a control freak destroys a stone's individuality. Every wall reflects the mason's art, but keeps that of the stone, too.

Consider Using Curves

A wall that curves is always a joy to see, if it's well done. Not only is it stronger, but if it blends with a slope or follows a contour, it looks as if it belongs where it is. A straight wall on a curving slope can never achieve this natural aspect. A curve *contains* something: space, soil, or another object like a planting, pool, flowing water, a patio.

Sometimes a freestanding wall curves around trees, boulders, grouped plantings, or a pool for a particularly attractive

A lookout point with flagstone floor marks the end of a drystone wall that curves with the hillside.

look. There should always be a visual reason for each curve. A wall that meanders on flat ground with nothing to wind around may be stronger, but its beauty is left with something missing. Just as a bend in a man-made garden watercourse should have a reason to exist, so should one in a wall. Feel free to "make something happen" or give that curve a reason to exist if it doesn't already have one.

The wall can come first. That concave section can be the place to build a pair of stone seats, install a pool, or plant a tree later. The curve contains whatever's there, no matter in which order it came.

Look to the Landscape

Arches and curved walls and stonework that let the stone stand out are all obviously man-made. But equally attractive is the boulder in a landscape where other elements are grouped around it, or the uncut stone slab that water flows over, then into a pool. Stones may be artfully placed in landscape settings, but they should always look as if they were there first. It's hard to find a truly ugly boulder, but some are certainly more visually pleasing than others. I look for lichens and surface texture in such accent stones. Gray granite is my favorite, with its rough, textured surface and its often weathered, irregular shapes.

HERE, I'D LIKE TO PAY TRIBUTE to an architect who truly understood the potential of stone in his work. The late Euinne Fay Jones, a native Arkansan like me, was also a stonemason. He used the native ledge sandstone around Fayetteville, Arkansas, in many of his houses, including his own.

As a young, eager stonemason, I was always appalled at how seldom that perfect building material was used in even the most elaborate of houses. I was spoiled by the bounty of that bold stone in the Ozark Mountains; no other place I have lived has had such easily accessible, easily workable stone. Yet so many other builders at that time failed to use this most natural of substances. Was it the lack of qualified labor necessary to do it right? It may have been ignorance, or short-term economics; for whatever reason, stone seemed to be the last choice for building material there. And when it *was* used, the workmanship was terrible: sloppy and mortar-smeared. I don't know which was worse — the lack of use or the poor use.

It took a man with Jones's insight to use that stone to its full potential. He understood that the cost was more than balanced by the longevity, zero upkeep, and beauty. He once described his method of getting the look he wanted this way: "First, I'd lay the stone myself, letting the mason help me. Then I'd help him lay stone. Then I could finally leave him to it."

I recently visited several of the Jones houses in and around Fayetteville with my friend the author/photographer, historian, and outdoorsman Ken Smith. With his guidance, I photographed some of these outstanding structures, always marveling at how well the architect knew his material. With the help of librarian Ellen Compton, we located some interior photographs that also show this man's genius with stone.

I had met Fay Jones only on two occasions, but as a young man I had recognized in him a rare appreciation for the use of stone and other natural materials in natural settings. The world will miss him.

point set at
this sharp c
stones. It is

For thick
a cross peen
mers are fas
Tomas Lipp
striking face
tool concent

The bus
face gives th
is even with
point, this h

The sto
the user att
maul, incre
more quick
often uneve
you don't v
with the tra
desired line

Pitchin
use. Its flat
the new cra
near the ed
(tapered ch
leave a hun
deeper. It re

Stone
Its principl
shattering l
in which yo
the point, a
until the sto
time to dre
leave lots o

Star dr
a point. It i
masonry bi
to create ho
for wooder

Drystone (unmortared) stone looks best in landscape work, since you're going for a natural look. Old, mortared walls can weather and be quite attractive, but they're best as contrasting elements to more natural features. In general, you'll want to keep that too disciplined look of mortared stone to a minimum outdoors, particularly in rural areas. Among its appealing characteristics, drystone stonework can convey an aspect of great age, which is one of the attractions of stone.

Of course, finely cut, symmetrically laid stonework can have great beauty. Certainly the temple walls of Machu Picchu are fascinating and stirring; so is the ashlar discipline of medieval castle walls and towers and the exact blocks of ancient Greece and Rome. The very permanence of stone has made us aware of the rightness of these examples over time.

For your own outdoor stone projects, I advise starting with drystone. You'll learn much more about stonework in general this way, and the end results will be more pleasing. If you should want or need to dismantle and/or move a wall or other structure later, it's a lot easier if the stones aren't mortared. That's a real consideration; I know competent masons who cringe when they see their first efforts and avoid showing them. With drystone, you can easily rework sections or whole projects once you've improved your skills.

The best advice I can give an aspiring mason who wants to keep tabs on the appearance of stonework in progress is to stand back and look at it frequently. Try to put yourself into the shoes of the casual observer. Does it look *right,* or is there something that nags at you, though you may not know what? Remember, every stone you set changes all the resulting options. If you're in doubt, don't just keep going; take a break, and seek the reactions of others whose opinions you trust. And if something you've done looks wrong, change it.

A Dry Stone Conservancy project, this culvert combines cut stone with fieldstone.

Basic too
and carbi
you need
A glove h
holding t

While pit
piece off
airborne.

A diamond-chip blade on a grinder can speed stone shaping by cutting grooves to be followed by chiseling. A dust mask must always be worn when creating stone dust; eye protection is also necessary.

Cutting tools. Stonecutting wheels are handy, from the small, 4-inch ones used on lightweight "sidewinder" grinders, to 7-inch wheels on circular saws, to really big diamond chip–embedded ones on chain-saw frames. While masonry wheels are available in grinderlike materials such as Carborundum, the diamond-chip ones cut quicker and last longer. These make smooth cuts and create a lot of dust. When I cut complete stone surfaces with these tools, I set the stones with the cut faces hidden to back or sides.

Miscellaneous Stone-handling Equipment

Here are a few more tools you should have on hand for any kind of stone-work project.

Wheelbarrow. Use a heavy-duty wheelbarrow for stonework. This is not the place for a bargain model; moving stone and mixing mortar will destroy a "handyman special" very soon. Avoid two-wheeled garden carts for heavy work; they're harder to control than a single-wheel wheelbarrow.

Digging bars. When you need to move stones around, it's best to use a metal bar to shift them. Using your hands to pry up stones is a good way to get your fingers smashed. You'll need a long digging bar (about 6 feet) for moving big stones around. A shorter one — about 3 feet long — is useful for working in tighter places.

Safety gear. Wear safety goggles. *Always.* A dust mask is also a good idea, to keep you from inhaling stone dust.

Worktable. Some masons work their stones on the ground, using knee pads. After hours of work, though, that can take its toll on the back. Take my advice and set your stones up on something so you won't have to bend down to shape them. A work table made of heavy wood is ideal. If a sharp drop in a bank of soil is handy, use that, although it will mean bending over more.

You can make a simple, functional table with two stacks of concrete blocks spanned by a 2- or 3-foot-long piece of 2×12. It will move around some, however. My favorite table has 3×3 legs, braced with 1×2 angle braces, with a 2-inch-thick top. A height of 24 to 30 inches high is ideal for most people, but you can adjust it to whatever's comfortable for you; just keep the table low enough to let you get a good swing with your hammer.

Drystone (unmortared) stone looks best in landscape work, since you're going for a natural look. Old, mortared walls can weather and be quite attractive, but they're best as contrasting elements to more natural features. In general, you'll want to keep that too disciplined look of mortared stone to a minimum outdoors, particularly in rural areas. Among its appealing characteristics, drystone stonework can convey an aspect of great age, which is one of the attractions of stone.

Of course, finely cut, symmetrically laid stonework can have great beauty. Certainly the temple walls of Machu Picchu are fascinating and stirring; so is the ashlar discipline of medieval castle walls and towers and the exact blocks of ancient Greece and Rome. The very permanence of stone has made us aware of the rightness of these examples over time.

For your own outdoor stone projects, I advise starting with drystone. You'll learn much more about stonework in general this way, and the end results will be more pleasing. If you should want or need to dismantle and/or move a wall or other structure later, it's a lot easier if the stones aren't mortared. That's a real consideration; I know competent masons who cringe when they see their first efforts and avoid showing them. With drystone, you can easily rework sections or whole projects once you've improved your skills.

The best advice I can give an aspiring mason who wants to keep tabs on the appearance of stonework in progress is to stand back and look at it frequently. Try to put yourself into the shoes of the casual observer. Does it look *right,* or is there something that nags at you, though you may not know what? Remember, every stone you set changes all the resulting options. If you're in doubt, don't just keep going; take a break, and seek the reactions of others whose opinions you trust. And if something you've done looks wrong, change it.

A Dry Stone Conservancy project, this culvert combines cut stone with fieldstone.

Making Stone Fit

When you're in the middle of a stonework project, you can't always stop to go hunt for the perfect stone to fill a particular spot. You'll have to cut and shape some of the stones you already have on hand, and that gets you into the core of the craft.

I know masons who shape every rock. Sometimes their work has too regular a look, in size and pattern; sometimes their skill camouflages their propensity to change the shape of every stone. I know others who shape stone only when necessary; their work looks less structured, more elegant, and more organic. Regardless of which path you choose, you'll need to have some tools ready to do the job.

Must-have Stonework Tools

For basic stonework, you can get away with two basic tools: a striking hammer and a chisel.

Currently, I use a 3-pound, one-piece, steel Estwing double-faced hammer. I also work with an old cross-peen (blunt chisel edge) head with the curved, shaped knob end of a single-bit hickory ax handle. The cross-peen weighs a few ounces less than the Estwing and I like the curve, which lets my wrist stay straighter.

My chisel of choice is actually called a tracer. It's a 2-inch-wide, carbide-tipped, steel Bicknel chisel that's 1¼ inches thick, with a square shank that has rounded corners. It started out about 9 inches long. Pounding on it has "mushroomed" the struck end; I've ground it off a few times, so now it's shorter. When you select a chisel for your own work, choose one at least 8 inches long to keep from bashing the knuckles of the hand that's holding it. You can save money by buying a steel chisel (without the carbide tip), but you'll need to sharpen it frequently if you do much stonecutting. You may want to get one with a wide rubber guard if your aim with that hammer isn't good.

More Specialized Stonework Tools

Here are some additional tools that will help in your work. You'll inevitably find them handy if you stick with this craft.

Hammers and mauls. For light work, the stone hammer, with its extended chisel

Basic tools — a striking hammer and carbide-tipped chisel — are all you need for most stone shaping. A glove helps protect the hand holding the chisel.

While pitching a stone, I cut a piece off the block, sending it airborne.

point set at a right angle to the handle, is quite useful. You can use either this sharp cutting edge or the striking face to knock off the edges of thin stones. It is most valuable for working brick or concrete block.

For thicker stones, consider a heavier hammer of 3 to 5 pounds, with either a cross peen or a straight peen parallel to the handle. With practice, these hammers are faster than the chisel, but they require more accuracy. Master mason Tomas Lipps has a heavy hammer that comes almost to a point opposite the striking face. It's a narrowed-down straight peen, actually. The weight of this tool concentrates the striking force in that narrow working face.

The bush hammer is used in dressing humps in stone. Its cross-hatched face gives the effect of multiple stone points. Each sharpened cutting point is even with the others, for a more uniform dressing appearance. Like the point, this hammer leaves distinctive patterns on the stone.

The stone maul is a blunt version of a wood-splitting maul. When the user attains a degree of accuracy, he or she can follow a line with the maul, increasing the force of the blows to break heavy, deep stones much more quickly than with a hammer and chisel. The break from the maul is often uneven, though, and sometimes the force will break the stone where you don't want it broken. The roughness can be dressed (smoothed out) with the tracer or pitching tool. Repeatedly hitting on the tracer along the desired line will also smooth the errant maul hits.

Pitching tool. The pitching tool is one that beginning masons seldom use. Its flat face, like a chisel that's had its edge ground off square, baffles the new craftsman. Its purpose is to drive the stone deeply when cutting near the edge, or pitching, as it's called, usually to a line. Where a tracer (tapered chisel) will spread the stone, often breaking out to the edge to leave a hump on the side, the pitching tool breaks the stone straighter and deeper. It requires harder blows, since it's moving more stone.

Stone point. The stone point is used to dress down humps in stone. Its principle is that of concentrating hammered blows in a very small area, shattering bits of stone at a time. Using the point follows a set-tap pattern in which you set the tool on a high spot while swinging the hammer, hit the point, and then set the point on a new spot to continue the process until the stone is smooth. When you establish a rhythm, it takes just a short time to dress even a sizable surface. Remember, though, that this tool will leave lots of marks on the stone's surface.

Star drill. A star drill is a four-fluted carbon steel tool that comes to a point. It is used to drill holes in stone. Largely superseded by modern masonry bits that are carbide-tipped, the star drill was used for centuries to create holes for anchoring bolts and gate-hinge pintles and latches and for wooden door and window jambs, among many other purposes.

Toru Oba uses a stone-cutting mallet, instead of a hammer, with his chisel. Many other sculptors also prefer to use mallets.

The stone point is hit by a hammer or mallet to dress humps in stones, leaving a stippled pattern.

Cutting tools. Stonecutting wheels are handy, from the small, 4-inch ones used on lightweight "sidewinder" grinders, to 7-inch wheels on circular saws, to really big diamond chip–embedded ones on chain-saw frames. While masonry wheels are available in grinderlike materials such as Carborundum, the diamond-chip ones cut quicker and last longer. These make smooth cuts and create a lot of dust. When I cut complete stone surfaces with these tools, I set the stones with the cut faces hidden to back or sides.

A diamond-chip blade on a grinder can speed stone shaping by cutting grooves to be followed by chiseling. A dust mask must always be worn when creating stone dust; eye protection is also necessary.

Miscellaneous Stone-handling Equipment

Here are a few more tools you should have on hand for any kind of stonework project.

Wheelbarrow. Use a heavy-duty wheelbarrow for stonework. This is not the place for a bargain model; moving stone and mixing mortar will destroy a "handyman special" very soon. Avoid two-wheeled garden carts for heavy work; they're harder to control than a single-wheel wheelbarrow.

Digging bars. When you need to move stones around, it's best to use a metal bar to shift them. Using your hands to pry up stones is a good way to get your fingers smashed. You'll need a long digging bar (about 6 feet) for moving big stones around. A shorter one — about 3 feet long — is useful for working in tighter places.

Safety gear. Wear safety goggles. *Always.* A dust mask is also a good idea, to keep you from inhaling stone dust.

Worktable. Some masons work their stones on the ground, using knee pads. After hours of work, though, that can take its toll on the back. Take my advice and set your stones up on something so you won't have to bend down to shape them. A work table made of heavy wood is ideal. If a sharp drop in a bank of soil is handy, use that, although it will mean bending over more.

You can make a simple, functional table with two stacks of concrete blocks spanned by a 2- or 3-foot-long piece of 2×12. It will move around some, however. My favorite table has 3×3 legs, braced with 1×2 angle braces, with a 2-inch-thick top. A height of 24 to 30 inches high is ideal for most people, but you can adjust it to whatever's comfortable for you; just keep the table low enough to let you get a good swing with your hammer.

Tools for Mortared Masonry

When you move on to stonework projects that involve mortar, you'll need to add other tools to your collection.

Trowel. The basic tool for mortared work is the trowel. Big ones have blades that are about 1 foot long; smaller, pointing trowels are about 4 inches long. They come in a wide range of shapes for specialized uses. The long, narrow ones are used mostly for laying concrete blocks, where you need long ridges of mortar on the block edges. Most stone-laying trowels are wider and often shorter. My favorite is about 8 inches long and 5 inches wide. The shorter length puts less strain on the wrist.

A trowel should be thin enough to be somewhat flexible. Brick and block masons cut with the edges of their trowels, but that's not a good idea in stonework. (Yes, it can work on thin, soft stones, but the trowel edge still suffers.) The mortar-pointing tool is very thin, used for pressing mortar into narrow spaces. Essentially, it's a trowel that's only a fraction of an inch wide. I use ¼-inch, ⅜-inch, and ½-inch pointers, depending on the tightness of the work I'm doing. I also use the pointer to rake (recess) the joints before the mortar is fully set. The blade of the pointer should flex, for smoother use.

Wire brush. A wire brush is handy for cleaning joints in mortared work, and for removing mud or clay from stones. It's also helpful for cleaning up shovels, mixing hoes, wheelbarrows, and other tools. (These always get mortar built up on them, which holds moisture and rusts the steel, and makes them heavier to use.)

Mixing hoe. Small mixing hoes, about the size of garden hoes, are useful for mixing small quantities of stone mortar. Large mixing hoes are fine for brick or block mortar, because this material is much wetter and easy to work, but are tough to work with on stone mortar.

Mortar mixer. A powered mortar mixer is good for larger jobs. Dump the prepared mortar into wheelbarrows to get it where it's needed, then let the mixer run with some water in it so what's left inside won't harden before you mix the next batch.

Basic mortaring tools are the trowel and the tuck pointer, for spreading the mortar and pushing it into spaces.

Stonecutting Basics

Now, let's take a look at the basic techniques you'll be using to cut and shape stones for just about any stonework project.

Flattening a Surface

Let's say the stone you need for whatever you're building is the right height to match the one next to it (so the next course of stone can cover the vertical joint) and the length is acceptable. But there's this bumped-out place that'll mess up the face if it's on the front, or hold the stone out too far if it's on the back side. To cut off the jutted-out edge of a stone, set the chisel where you want it, then lean it out away from the edge a little. If you hold the chisel vertically, the stone will probably just chip out, leaving a hump that's hard to remove. By leaning the chisel out at a 5-degree angle to the rock surface, the cut is apt to go deeper, which is what you want.

Holding the chisel at the appropriate angle, hit the chisel lightly at first to trace a line in the stone. Then go over the line again, hitting harder.

QUARRYING STONE – THEN AND NOW

HISTORICALLY, THE PRINCIPAL USE OF A STAR DRILL was to drill holes in a line for quarrying stone. When these holes were drilled, by repeatedly sledge-hammering the tool, the stone was ready for one of two major treatments.

Sometimes wooden pins were driven into the drilled holes, then water was dripped onto them. As the wood swelled, the pressure increased evenly down the line of holes. Eventually, the stone split. This usually took time.

The other, more frequently used approach entailed feathers and wedges. Half-round metal "feathers" were inserted in the holes, leaving slots between them. Iron wedges were then driven into these spaces, with the stonecutter striking evenly down the line and then repeating. This technique split the stone much more quickly than the wooden-plug treatment.

I've watched stone ledges being quarried for crushed stone using this drilled-hole method, with a modern twist. Jackhammers are used: compressed-air-driven impact drivers with hardened steel bits. Then the line of holes is filled with explosives and the rock is blasted. The pieces are then run through a rock crusher to produce gravel.

The force of the "shot rock" technique often creates cracks throughout the stone, weakening it. For crushed stone, this isn't a problem. But for masonry and sculpture, avoid shot rock, for obvious reasons. The feathers and wedges are still the best way to go for our purposes.

Kevin Fife still splits granite with traditional feathers and wedges (above) for an antique look (below).

Repeat until the stone cuts. This is called pitching, no matter which tool you use. Sometimes it'll take just one hit, sometimes many. At times, all you'll get will be some chips out to the edge and a lot of frustration. Don't spend forever on a stone that doesn't want to be cut.

If you're cutting a wide stone, say to get a certain width for a wall, trace one side of the hump by hitting with the chisel to make a line, then measure and trace the other side to match. Trace both edges, too. Now hit along all these lines until the stone cuts. You can cut an 8- or 10-inch-thick stone in perhaps 10 minutes, depending on conditions and your stamina.

Inevitably you'll try to get a flat plane on a stone that isn't flat and you'll end up with chipped edges and a rounded hump in the middle. This can be avoided by leaning the chisel as we said, or by using the pitching tool. It drives the stone better, causing it to break deep instead of splitting out to the edge. But quite often you'll still have that hump, and if it's important to flatten it, it'll take more work. Set the stone with the hump on top so you can get at it better. Angle the chisel into the stone where the rise of the hump starts and cut into it. If the angle is too flat, the chisel won't bite. If it's too vertical, nothing much will happen, or the whole stone will eventually break. With practice, a few hits will lift off a sizable chunk, which will, however, fly up toward your face. You will be glad for the safety goggles, even though you might lose some nose skin. Continue working by going around the hump, aiming for more places to get the chisel to bite and lift off more chunks, to leave a face on the stone.

Another method is to turn up the chisel edgeways and cut a groove across the face of the hump. Then use that cut to set the chisel in, to cut both ways out from it.

Either way, there *will* be chisel marks, which will last approximately forever. I prefer to keep the natural faces of the stones showing and hide my cuts at sides, top, bottom, and back. If you must cut a face of the stone that's going to be visible, you can carefully grind out those marks.

If this face of the stone isn't to be seen, you can speed up the operation by using a diamond-embedded cutting blade on a grinder to cut grooves across the face of the objectionable hump. I use a small "sidewinder" grinder with a 4-inch blade to score these cuts, and then chip them out with the chisel.

Keep in mind that mechanized cutting and chiseling causes more dust (and noise) than hand cutting. The resultant cloud of rock dust can give you silicosis or worse problems, so be sure to wear a dust mask. If you're working around other people, you may also want to use a mist of water from a

The stone point is used here with a set-tap repetition to dress down a high place on the stone.

hose as you cut, to help control the dust. I usually try to hand-shape only, leaving the meaner stones for use only if I run out of good ones. Then I bring out the grinder and set up away from people while I attack the stones.

Dividing and Splitting Stone

Cutting thin stones, particularly sandstone, is a challenge. It's a little like cutting glass: it breaks where it wants to, not where you plan it. Even if you've traced both faces of a flat stone, it'll have a tendency to break somewhere else. Setting a thin stone in a bed of sand before you attempt to split it helps, because the sand absorbs the jolts that do the damage. If the edges won't show, you can score deeply with the grinder on both faces and then break the stone.

Splitting or breaking a large rock to get two or more manageable pieces usually takes more than a hammer and chisel. Here's where a stone maul is handy. Weighing anywhere from 4 to 18 pounds, it's a serious tool. Trace a line as you would with the hammer and chisel, then go over it again and again, hitting harder each time. Hit in the right place enough times and any stone will eventually give up. Aim is important, though, or you may end up shattering the stone and having to start all over. Here's where a generous rock pile will supply another candidate for you to practice your shaping skills to fill that space.

You will discover an extremely annoying tendency for a stone you've worked on forever to break wrong just as you apply that last, exacting hit. That's usually because there was a fracture hidden there, and pounding on the rock made it let go. If a stone has visible fractures in it, like crazing in pottery, don't try to shape it before you use it. Better yet, don't even bring it home. Leave it in the woods for the snakes to live under; they don't care much.

Splitting begins with finding grain, then tracing a line across each face of the stone. Mark the line with repeated blows with a chisel. The stone will split along the traced line if the grain has been read correctly.

STONE-SHAPING SAFETY

SAFETY IS A MUST IN STONECUTTING because the work is inherently hazardous. Knuckles get skinned, fingers get smashed by rocks, and sharp pieces fly around a lot. Flying chips are a real potential danger — they can cut you or damage your eyes if you forget your goggles. Another common hazard in stonecutting is missing the chisel with the hammer, but not missing the hand holding it.

When you're cutting or shaping stone, always wear a heavy glove on the hand you use to hold the chisel. It doesn't provide much protection from a missed blow (that'll hurt with or without a glove), but it does guard your knuckles from the sharp edge that's left when the chisel takes off a piece of stone.

Advanced Shaping Techniques

Beyond relatively simple stonecutting and shaping for good, tight work, there's a world of advanced creativity in stone that approaches sculpture. I'm reminded of the Peruvian water-carrying channels in stone, fit so tightly together that they didn't leak. Such mating of stone surfaces requires a lot more than rough cutting. If small enough, stones were sometimes rubbed against each other until almost polished. Or abrasives, such as sand, were rubbed against the stone, often with water.

The drilled holes in the roof gable stones of Machu Picchu were supposedly done with bamboo twirled against the stone in a stream of sand-laden water. A similar approach was used with the soapstone found in Schuyler, Virginia, to cut it for the countertops and myriad other uses before commercial substitutes were developed. Flat steel blades, with no teeth, were drawn back and forth through the stone while steady streams of water with sand were poured onto it. A modern version of this method utilizes extreme high-pressure jets of water laden with sand. (We're talking many thousands of pounds per square inch here.) The results are clean cuts in even the hardest stone. Such machinery is, of course, very expensive and not very portable.

Cemetery stones get their high polish with a series of steps. The stone is cut, often with oversize diamond chip–embedded saw blades, then

Skilled shaping can happen with primitive methods; these stone protrusions on Machu Picchu structures were created with careful pounding of hammerstones.

Toru Oba's awe-inspiring patio uses 5-inch-thick granite slabs. He left and cut deliberate holes between the close fits for plantings, and used rough-surface accent flagstones.

ground smooth. Increasingly fine abrasives are then used, ending with extremely fine polishing rouge, applied much like the rubbing compound used to finish automotive paint.

Stone is sometimes even turned on lathes similar to wood or metal turnings. Round ornamental tops for entryway columns are done this way, and sometimes other rounded shapes, such as the columns themselves, are turned. It's fascinating to watch a commercial stoneyard operation handling this hard substance as if it were soft wood.

Sculpture has always consisted of rough shaping, then finer chiseling, smoothing, and polishing. Dense, soft stone, like marble, works well for sculpture, while a crumbly stone would be a disaster. It is always amazing to learn that ancient sculptors could do so much with absolutely no mechanized tools. Time and skill were the keys. I'm reminded of the steps cut into solid white granite at Machu Picchu, and the big blocks with protruding shafts, as in the "Hitching Post of the Sun" atop the highest temple there.

Advanced stonecutting is challenging, but can result in some spectacular work. Master mason Toru Oba, of Albemarle County, Virginia, cut round holes in 5-inch-thick, quarried granite slabs for a patio near Charlottesville. The holes were for eventual plantings, and were cut with masonry bits drilling the perimeters of the circles, which were then knocked out, chiseled, and ground smooth. These slabs were then fitted exactly at their random edges to each other and bedded dry on crushed gravel. In other places on the same estate, Toru cut and fitted flagstone steps to existing irregular outcroppings of granite.

George Gonzalez, another master mason, of the San Francisco area, has made the worked faces of his stones his signature. The designs of chisel cuts become art in themselves, and, instead of detracting from the look of the stone, enhance it. There's a similarity to the hammerstone marks in the Peruvian stonework, telling how it was done.

A public fountain in Santa Fe, New Mexico, that George and Stone Foundation founder Tomas Lipps built a generation ago is a striking example of the modern stonemason's art, featuring different treatments of stone faces. There are several types of stone, and some of the faces are smooth, some are weathered, and some have those distinctive cut marks.

Such work requires a great deal of time, extensive effort, and masterful skill — an achievement we can all strive for.

Fountainhead Rock, a public fountain in Santa Fe, was built by George Gonzalez, Tomas Lipps, and Michel Giannesini.

DON'T PLAY THE GUESSING GAME

WHEN SHAPING STONE or selecting the right one in its natural state, measure both the rock and the space where it's going. (Make sure you allow for the joint, as well, in mortared work.) Otherwise, you're all too likely to select a stone that's larger than the available space, or to cut it to the wrong dimensions. It's a common phenomenon in stonework. Maybe we see spaces as bigger than solids; I don't know. But if you watch beginning masons, you'll see them repeatedly trying to fit oversize rocks into undersize spaces.

Learn to measure, or to allow for more space. You don't need to bother with a tape measure; just do it by hand — literally. With my stubby fingers, I know it's 7 inches from outstretched thumb tip to index finger tip, and that's how I measure stone. When I do use a tape measure, it inevitably gets grit in it, or it gets dropped and lost, or it gets a large stone dropped on it, especially if it's new and costly. Measure your hand once and remember the result, then you'll never be without your "handy" measuring guide.

Ｆor the beginner, a path or patio is a good project. When the guidelines are followed, these relatively simple projects can result in attractive stonework and

Paths and Patios

provide good training. You may use the stone in its natural shapes and make a puzzlelike pattern, do minimal shaping and cutting to take away the odd shape, or buy dimensional, precut stone.

Begin with the best-shaped stones you can get, to minimize frustration. You can go on to odder shapes later, as you gain proficiency and want to challenge yourself.

LEFT: This stone patio incorporates existing boulders into the design and creates a visual bridge between the backyard and the landscape beyond it.

Choosing Stone for Flatwork

The term *flagstone* refers to relatively thin stones laid flat, creating a clean and durable surface to walk, ride, or drive on. Working with flagstones is called "flatwork" by masons. Flagstone can be almost any kind of stone. Granite is wonderful, but you'll almost never find smooth pieces in nature. Commercially cut granite will give you that smoothness, and sometimes that's what you want. Smooth, cut stone can be a welcome addition to natural stone, providing variety in texture and appearance.

You can also buy rough-quarried granite that has been split as the ancient masons split it, with drilled holes, "feathers," and wedges driven in along a line until the stone cracks. (You've probably seen traces of these holes at the edges of old stones used in commercial building foundations or in city retaining walls.) You'll need to dress the split faces, though, because they're typically too irregular for use as flagstones.

Sandstone is my favorite material for flagstone. We find it on top of the ground in the West Virginia mountains. Sometimes it's split off in slabs by natural forces: a soft place erodes, water gets in and freezes, or maybe tree roots take hold, and the stones crack apart. These natural splits tend to have a level but rough surface that won't get slick underfoot when wet, so I like them for walkways and steps.

Sandstone is easy to cut and shape, and its variety of shades and colors keeps it from fading in large expanses. It's also relatively light in weight, which makes it easier to manhandle into place. (Igneous stones such as granite and basalt usually don't come in naturally thin slabs and these thicker stones are harder to manage.)

Now, really soft sandstone isn't good as flagstone. It will erode in a few years and break easily. Many old walkways, steps, and even walls have stones so eroded they're almost gone. For your work, go for the medium to hard grades of sandstone, which you can identify by looking for the finer crystals or by cutting into it.

Like sandstone, limestone is a sedimentary rock, so it's naturally layered and makes good flags. Limestone doesn't have the range of colors sandstone has, but it cuts well and is denser than sandstone.

Slate is used quite a bit now in entryways and mudrooms. It's invariably thin, and should be mortar-set so as not to break or split in use. If I were to use slate in large expanses, I'd want it at least 2 inches thick and set on a concrete or a deep, packed gravel base. Slate is dark, and it will eat up the light in any room, as can other types of

Both of these can be used as flagstones. The top one has been cut to shape; the bottom stone can be set into the ground as is or split along its noticeable grain.

dark stone. That's a problem we have with our soapstone floor. We painted the ceiling off-white between the overhead beams to try to lighten that room; French doors also let in sunlight on the south face of the house. Once we covered part of the floor with a light rug, but we never liked how the rug changed the character of the room. We eventually added light-colored furniture and more lamps, and that mostly solved the problem.

Unfortunately, soapstone is now expensive since its production for countertops and other flat surfaces has all but been replaced with man-made products, so it isn't quarried in large quantities. It is now a specialty stone, although still a viable option for flatwork. (School and industrial laboratories still prefer soapstone, as it is so resistant to chemicals.)

Bluestone is flat sandstone, and is currently highly favored for flatwork. It's sold by the square foot when precut into easily applied and commonly desired dimensions (from 1×1-foot to 3×3-foot pieces, and larger). Most stoneyards sell it by the ton if it's left in its natural shapes. The principal objection I have to this stone is its thinness and, therefore, its instability. It's normally available 1 inch thick, although I special-order it at least 1½ inches thick.

These squared flagstones have been complemented with creek pebbles set on edge for a study in texture.

Flagstone Pathways

The simplest use of flagstone is in paths where each stone floats in gravel, like stepping-stones. These aren't fitted to each other or to the sides of the path. They are underlaid with gravel or crushed stone to let rainwater percolate down below freezing level if possible, so frost won't heave them. Even if frost does move them, the stones go back roughly to their old positions afterward, because there are no joints that can be knocked out of place.

Choosing the Stones

Look for smoothness when choosing this type of pathway stone. Often a thin stone looks good, but its surface is warped, which can cause folks to trip. Dips hold water, which can freeze in winter and make a path dangerous. Keep in mind that smooth shouldn't mean slick or the walkway will become a hazard when wet. The surface should be rough enough to keep feet from slipping but not so rough that it creates problems. Even with all of these points to keep in mind, choosing stones for flags can be easier than

selecting them for other projects. You need only one ideal surface to each rock here, because you'll see and walk on only one side.

The thickness of path stones can vary a lot, but I like a minimum of 2 inches, so the stones won't break or get pushed around. Always get large flagstones; small stones (less than about 1 foot square) tend to tip when people walk on them.

Note that any flat stone will fool you into thinking it's smooth, so it's a good idea to check the faces, maybe with a straightedge, to make sure they are smooth enough. Use a chisel to take down larger humps. A stone point works better on smaller raised areas. Another way to do limited smoothing is to use a diamond-chip blade at an angle and sweep across the rough places. If you're careful, you can avoid the circular marks this leaves. You will hear of laying flagstone rough with the idea of using a terrazzo machine to smooth it later. That will work, but it's costly, takes forever, makes clouds of dust, and leaves an unnatural ground-down surface.

Individual Stepping-stones

Flagstone, by definition, is thin. For outdoor projects, though, thick stones and irregular-shaped stones can be used, just as long as there is one good face for the top. Here's the place to use those three-dimensional triangles, parallelograms, and other crazy chunks that won't work anywhere else. Just dig out a hole for each stone and set it firmly in place on gravel, packing more gravel around it to keep it stable.

Another good way to use deeper, thicker stones is as stepping-stones across a stream or shallow pond. Flat stones set on crushed rock here will settle as the base erodes or the soil underneath softens. But deeply set stones, with those necessarily flat tops, will stay put.

Setting a stone in shallow water is done the same way as on soil; you just get your feet wet in the process. In either case, dig down and use crushed stone as the base so it won't compact or wash away. A 4- to 6-inch base is usually deep enough. Use coarser gravel in water; the finer stuff won't stay, and as it washes, the stones will settle.

I have seen flagstones as thick as 8 inches, set deep and stable. And I've seen ½-inch-thick stones just waiting for someone to step on an edge and tip the stone. Follow

Geometric stone shapes and gravel offset plantings in a thoroughly modern design.

the above general directions, and you can create some wonderful places to spend time outdoors (or in). Just don't destroy your back doing it.

Preparing the Base for a Pathway

Simple stepping-stone paths are charming, but for high-traffic areas, a more carefully laid pathway is probably a better choice. Bedding pathway stones directly on the soil is a big mistake: the area won't drain well, and the stones will settle and tilt. Many masons lay a concrete slab first, for any and all flagstone work. They bed the stone in wet mortar and fill the joints with mortar. That's fine if you want or can live with the expense, but a good, dry-laid walkway set on a gravel base will stay when done right.

The gravel for such a walkway should be crushed stone, not round creek gravel. Rounded edges never pack tightly and always let high heels sink in. The rounded fill will also work away from the stones, leaving stone edges standing up enough to trip over. (If you do end up with this problem, top-dressing with rock dust or fine sand will help, because the finer particles will fill the spaces between the larger gravel pieces and stabilize them.)

For most outdoor flagstone paths, dig out a 3- to 4-foot-wide area that's 6 to 12 inches deep. (Ideally you should dig down below the frost line.) Fill with the fine crushed stone, leaving the surface of the gravel about 2 inches (or whatever the average thickness is for your chosen stones) below the final level of the path.

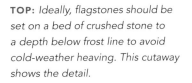

TOP: *Ideally, flagstones should be set on a bed of crushed stone to a depth below frost line to avoid cold-weather heaving. This cutaway shows the detail.*

RIGHT: *Level flagstones to eliminate high and low spots.*

STONE STYLE: Paths

For a casual look, place your chosen stones on the gravel randomly, or in any loose design you want. Dig thicker stones in deeper so the top of the path will be even. (Set each stone with just a little slope to it, to shed water.)

It is a good idea to give this kind of pathway some sort of border, perhaps with smaller stones of any length. Set these on edge so their depth in the ground will hold them in place. Without a border, soil and gravel will work into each other over time, and grass will invade the path, covering its edges.

A variation here is to select stones with straight outside edges and let them define the borders. The effect isn't the same, since the flags won't float free of the edges, but it's a pattern you may like.

For a more closely set flagstone path, fit the stones together, with about a 1-inch joint between. You'll do a lot of searching, or a lot of cutting, to get this close fit. Again, you should use the largest stones you can get and/or handle for the center of the pathway. You can get away with some stones smaller than 1 square foot if you place them at the edges, where they'll bear less weight and suffer less wear.

Cutting flagstone can be frustrating. Because the stone is thin, pounding on it with a hammer and chisel often causes it to break, not where you've been trimming a crooked edge smooth, but back near the center, where you want it left in one piece. Here's where a cutting blade helps. Score both sides about ⅜ inch deep and break off the edge protrusions with a hammer. If you're cutting near the center, prop up both sides and bump the scored line with a large wooden block, like the end of a 6-foot-long 2×6. Or set a narrow piece of wood, like a 2×2, under the score line and tap off the overhanging part while you stand on the rest. You can cut flagstones entirely with the chisel, but you'll get more bad breaks that way. Sometimes you can lessen the tendency to break off too much by chiseling the edge from the side instead of from the top or bottom.

There's plenty of room for your artful expression in a path like this. A lot of people like squares and rectangles only; others like random shapes and sizes but want straight-line joints. Still others want the stones to be totally random, even down to matching very irregular edges. Depending on how formal the path is to be, any of these will work, but each is a different style of stonework.

ABOVE LEFT: Todd Campbell creates impromptu arches from found stone while hiking.

ABOVE RIGHT: Coarsely shaped stone creates a colorful veneer.

OPPOSITE: Todd Campbell lays coquille siltstone and dry-stack basalt in coarse sand to provide excellent drainage.

"I live in a town so remote, it was the last place in all forty-eight continental states to have mail service delivered by mule" is how Todd Campbell describes his Utah home, where he has spent most of his life. "Southern Utah is all about the rockscape." This setting both inspired Todd's vocation and quickly informed his personal aesthetic, which is vehemently "anything *but* traditional," he says. "I most like stonework that isn't overly controlling, that lets the spontaneous nature of rock, and not the inclinations of the mason, remain its most compelling virtue."

Todd roots for any underdog, a philosophy that extends to his choice of material: he buys stone from other masons and builders that they have rejected, and devises techniques and applications for incorporating these castoffs. "Living in a cow town," he says, "people can't afford quarried stone, so my challenge is to work with found stone" and still concoct a highly polished result. "There's a colloquialism here [about requiring] adaptation to what's available: 'Make do to get done.' " Local stone includes a blue-black manganese ironstone, a red sandstone, a blond siltstone (which requires flintknapping techniques to shape successfully), and a black basalt that generally comes in big "pillow-shaped" forms. Todd often uses what might be considered primitive stoneshaping techniques, including flintknapping (using a hammerstone or the billet of an antler

to shape a stone) and other stone-on-stone techniques to render what he says is a "much more human product than the predictably sized/shaped/rendered stone shaped by steel tools. I've learned to appreciate a degree of refinement in my masonry that reflects coarser, more natural function and fit than many other masons' work."

Acknowledging the spatial dynamic of stonework, Todd suggests that the mark of a good mason is the ability to see "problem rocks and solution rocks. It's imperative," he says, "that a mason quarry or collect his own rock, for that purpose." He cites Bob Marley (who in turn is citing the Bible) that " 'the stone that the builder refused becomes the head cornerstone.' It can transform a project." As an example, he once found a "miracle stone" — a basalt boulder that he was shocked to discover had a sun spot in its shadow when he lifted it; somehow it was pierced all the way through. Todd convinced his client to feature its uniqueness by making it a focal water-collection basin for a fountain. Another technique he employs with stones too thin to be laid flat is *coquillé,* or a cracked-eggshell effect, which involves turning them on edge and driving them into the sand.

A mason, Todd says, is someone who brings his or her "horse sense to a problem and engineers a solution." He admits that he likes to push the rules, and even creates techniques that defy traditional drystone philosophy — such as "slip-form" masonry, a technique that works especially well when you have "rocks so ugly you don't know which side to bury in the mud," he says, laughing. In this case, smooth cobbles and ultra-angular rocks alike can be mortared together to take the shape of any temporary formwork, "with little regard to plumb, square, or level," Todd says.

Function, durability, and beauty are the points of the stonemason's triangle. A mason whose design encompasses all these elements has "one eye on the micro and one on the macro," he says, making the work both engrossing and satisfying. Todd relishes projects that keep him up at night, scratching his head about things like how to make sure the substructure that he spontaneously devised is anchored properly. He also loves ribbing the drystone purists, arguing that "a stone can fit to a stone, but also to the intention of what's being built." For this Utah craftsman, there's beauty in the most surprising things.

Setting Pathway Stones

Regardless of the pattern you choose, it's important to bed each stone carefully, to get a uniform height. It's tempting to raise a low edge with just a handful of gravel under it, but that leaves a hollow under the stone that will settle in time. Make sure each stone contacts the bedding evenly, so it'll stay where you want it. Even when you set the stones carefully, variations in the surface might leave joints with high edges to trip over. Cut these down with a chisel to get as even a thickness as you can at the joint. Cutting from the side will take a high place down to more of a bevel or slope at this edge.

Filling the Joints

I usually don't grout with mortar outdoors, because any buckling will crack the joints. Mortar grout also keeps rainwater from soaking on down through the gravel and away from the stones. You'll almost always have places where the water stands, making the stones slick, and when it freezes, it's even worse.

CONSIDERING COBBLESTONES

COBBLESTONES WERE USED IN THE ROMAN EMPIRE as a practical road covering. As small as 4 inches square and usually 8 to 12 inches tall, cobbles are stones in manageable sizes cut to close-fitting rectangular shapes and set on end to provide more strength and wear-resistance. When set on a base of gravel or crushed stone, cobbles make a very good surface. They were invariably used in regions where cheap or slave labor made their quarrying, cutting, and installation economical.

Cobblestones were often torn up when streets were rebuilt for modern traffic, and surpluses collected all over Europe. These often found their way to the United States as ships' ballast. They are expensive today, as stone goes, and each covers very little space. Cobblestones are still laid today as in the past, with no grouting. Often they're used in patterns around fountains, in courtyards, or as paths, but sometimes they're laid horizontally to form borders for walkways or flower beds.

To fill the joints, I use the same type of crushed stone as for the fill but finer, with rock dust in it (it's called "crusher-run" at the quarry) to finish the joints. Plain rock dust works well too, and it's easy to sweep it into the joints with a broom. Grass will get a start in this fine material, but it can't get far in a 1-inch joint. You can leave it, or else kill it with an herbicide, boiling water, or a weed flamer. Very low-growing ground covers can work well along and among stones in a pathway like this; see what your local nursery has to offer.

Paths with Steps

Paths are great landscaping features. A path should lead to surprises if possible, and be an adventure in itself. It should never be straight if you can help it. It should bend around accents, such as boulders, ponds, and plantings, to make it look as if they were there first.

Paths should also be able to climb slopes if they're there, and if the slope is even a little steep, you'll need steps. A step that's a maximum of 7 inches high (the riser) and a minimum of 16 inches deep (the tread) is easy to walk up or down. Avoid steeper risers or shallower treads; don't make your steps an endurance trial.

When laying out steps in landscaping, it's best to group them for getting from one level to the next. Unless it's necessary, don't have one step, then only a few feet to the next one. A person walking that path will fail to anticipate these and stumble, or will concentrate so much he will miss

The ideal stone step is one piece, whatever its shape or style, for appearance and stability.

the features around him. Group two to four steps at a time, with a rail if you find it necessary, then leave longer stretches of comparatively level path (assuming the grade will allow it). A stone seat near a set of steps makes a welcome resting place.

Basic Step Construction

The simplest stone step is a single, 7-inch-thick flagstone. Lacking that, you'll have to build your steps from smaller stones. Piecing a tread has to be done carefully in drystone *or* mortared work. A small stone at the front of the tread will eventually dislodge, so don't use one there. If I piece a step tread, I like to do it with only two stones, but you can fudge that. It's most important in steps to make sure everything stays stable, because a fall is farther from a step than from an unstable stone on the flat. Sometimes when I have to use three stones for a tread, I use two side by side that come together at the front, even if the space between them widens out in a triangle as it goes back. The three-sided middle stone used as a filler won't extend to the lip of the tread, and so will stay put. From a construction standpoint, two rectangles would give the most stability when piecing treads, but too many of these may look boring. For variety, one tread stone can be larger, and the joint between them doesn't have to be straight; angle the joint, or fit one stone to the natural edge of the other.

Fitting treads. These tread stones should be fitted tightly to each other with little gravel fill, or it'll wash out. If you're mortaring the steps, don't recess the grout. And if you have too high humps on the treads, cut them down smooth. I've almost turned an ankle on steps that were natural shapes, with treads varying as much as 3 inches. That's not a flight of steps; it's an obstacle course.

SPECIAL TIPS FOR MORTARED STEPS

IF YOU WANT MORTARED STEPS, you're going to have to excavate the whole area and pour a below-frost-line footing. Since it's not holding up a large structure, this footing can be just the size of the steps, plus the two side walls, without the extensions necessary for a chimney or building foundation. When I do steps this way, I use one of two options. I may lay up the bulk of the space back and up, behind the steps themselves, with concrete block or rough stones. Then I build the actual steps on this rising base. More often, I lay the first tread, either the one-height stone (or side-by-side one-height stones) or two layers. Then I fill behind that with stone chunks or mortar until I'm level all the way back, as the base for the next riser. In mortared work, I'll extend the treads to form bases for the side walls. With mortar, you get a little slack in piecing the treads, but remember never to use a small stone (one less than about 12 inches square) to form the front lip of the step.

You can form up concrete steps, or even buy them precast, have them set, and veneer them with stone. That would let you overhang the tread if you wanted that look. You can do that anyway, but it means all the tread stones have to be the same thickness, which is demanding. I don't like veneered steps, because water tends to get behind the stones and freeze, popping them off. I don't do them unless I'm extending a thin-stone patio or path onto the steps with the same material. Once I did build up the risers so another mason who was laying a 1-inch-thick cut-stone patio could set the same stone as treads. He was bedding in crusher-run, but that thin stone wouldn't have worked as dry-laid steps.

Stone Steps

A 3-foot-wide set of stone steps will fit nicely with most paths and is easy to build. The stones you use must be flat and heavy enough to stay in place under foot traffic. It is very important to wedge stones, if necessary, so they are stable — a rocking stone step is very dangerous. As with flagstones, don't be misled by nice wide slabs of stone that aren't smooth on top. And remember that only the top surface and leading edge are visible in the finished product.

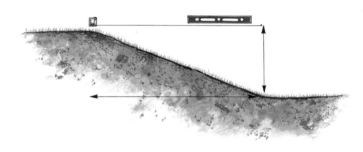

[**1**] First, estimate the slope by measuring its height from a level, allowing 16 in. for each tread and 6–7 in. for each riser.

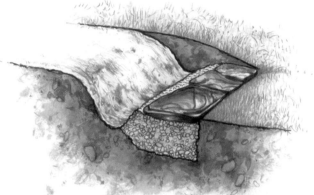

[**2**] Dig into the slope to extend an almost level place back about 18 in. and 36 in. wide. Dig down 4 to 6 in. and fill with crushed gravel to just below grade. Lay wide stones, the full 18 in. deep — do not piece stones for the depth of the tread. Use no more than two stones across the 36 in. width of the steps. Smaller stones would tip, rock, settle, and slant. Place the stones rough-side down and dig out for irregularities.

[**3**] Dig back at the height of the top of this step for the next one. Lay these second-step stones (again, no more than two) so as to avoid a running joint. Let the front edges of these stones overlap the backs of the first step stones by an inch or two. Since these back edges will be covered, place the stones so that any rough or uneven edges are here. Shape as necessary, but try to start with good, flat, rectangular stones.

[**4**] Dig out for the third step, just as you did for the others, then lay the final stones, avoiding running joints. Don't shorten the depth of outdoor treads to meet the slope. Less than 16 in. is awkward to negotiate.

Now, these tread stones won't all be that magical 7-inch thickness unless you've searched a long time and/or paid a lot of money. If one is thicker, you can dig it into the ground to leave the right height. If it's too thin, lay a substantial stone under it to bring it to height. Avoid using small stones to raise the tread stones, because rainwater running off the tread will get under there, eroding the base and loosening the step.

Building up. Build any flight of stone steps from the bottom up. If you have a deep tread stone, the back part can form the base for the next riser. If that next riser/tread combination needs to be dug in, you'll have to cut off the back of the existing tread at the 16-inch dimension before you proceed. Slope each tread a half inch or so down to the front so water won't stand in dips on the surface.

Adding borders. If you don't border stone steps, dirt will wash onto them and grass will invade them. You may not mind that at all. But it's neater to build a wall up both sides of your steps to edge them and to keep the rest of nature off them — and to show off your good stonework too, of course. Use the basic guidelines for a drystack wall here (see page 94), but you'll step it up often, as the risers go up. Set each first-course stone into the ground firmly, and/or fill up to it on the outside. You're actually building two miniature retaining walls alongside your steps, going up a steep slope. I like to grade the soil on either side of the step walls to create a more natural look.

Most landscape steps are the same width as the path: 3 to 4 feet. If you lay up the side walls another foot thick, you have a substantial structure in your flight of steps. It takes time. Most masons figure all the step surfaces when they estimate such a project, then add a hefty percentage because it's such demanding work.

Curved Steps

A pleasant variation on the basic set of landscape steps is to curve them. This usually works best with an outward, radial curve, to direct foot traffic from both sides or several parts of the garden. It requires little more effort than straight steps and is a lot more interesting. You'll have to shape the treads somewhat, but the wider the flight of steps and the less the curve, the less cutting each individual stone will need. Let the sides of the set of steps taper inward as they go up, toward an imaginary converging point, to direct people to a single pathway or other destination above.

My son, Charlie, and I built these steps of gathered fieldstone. They curve up alongside the client's house, through a retaining wall that surrounds the family's swimming pool.

Wide, curved steps such as these invite foot traffic and direct it up to a goal: path, seats, plantings, water feature. Their effect is inclusive.

Circular steps like this can also have a real structure at the focal point above, such as a pool, a boulder, or a planting. The path at the top would divide around the feature, then either join behind it or head off in two different directions.

Patios

A patio follows the same principles as a flagstone path. It can be set on concrete or gravel, but it should have a slight pitch to it to shed water better. (The same 1-inch-in-8-feet slope that many porch floors have will work here; it's enough to shed water but not enough to be noticeable.) Although a pathway can undulate with the terrain, the patio should stay even, so you'll definitely want to use a level on each stone to keep everything straight.

I like to walk on any gravel-bedded flagstone for several days before I grout (fill between the stones) to complete any settling. It would seem obvious that you could use a powered compactor to get all the base level, but that doesn't work, because the thickness of each stone varies, and you'll still have to dig down to accommodate the thicker ones. You can tap a stone down a very little with a wooden block, but don't count on that much. If a stone goes down too far, pry it up and add gravel underneath. After it has stabilized, fill the joints.

Patio shape is such a matter of individual taste, it's hard to give any guidelines here. Sometimes the landscape can give you ideas: if there's a terrace, for instance, follow its contour. If you're lucky enough to have a watercourse, either man-made or natural, follow its curve with one side of the patio. Property lines, retaining walls, woods edges, and slopes can also serve as boundaries to define the patio's shape. You may want to make the entire patio a series of paths in flagstone, circling around other features. Make the paths just prevalent enough to suggest they're part of a whole, but have lots of room for plants, accent stones, pools, seats, and steps, too.

Geometric shapes can also provide inspiration for your patio. A strictly square or rectangular patio is fine and easy to lay out, but pretty boring. Plantings and accent boulders can look great here, visually softening sharp corners and straight edges. You could even leave planting holes here and there within the patio itself. For a focal point, you could place a big, mossy boulder off to one side a bit and build the patio to it. Visitors will invariably want to see what is behind the boulder, so add a little flagstone around the outside of it so people can walk there.

A circle is always an appealing shape and can make for an interesting patio. Have the stones radiating out from a center, which itself can be a raised bed (framed with more stonework, of course). Or leave a circle of earth in the center in which to plant a dwarf tree. Don't get something that'll grow so big the roots will buckle the stones. Good gardeners (and I am not one) have a knack for planting several shrubby things together, so that one or another is blooming during most of the season.

Even in the most structured patio, surprises, such as this angled oasis in stone and greenery, are welcome additions.

STONE STYLE: Patios

Patio styles range as far as the imagination. Their common goal, though, is to create a (more or less) structured space that's apart from lawn or woods or other natural surroundings. This space should be defined, in any way you choose — a separate space to be experienced.

Geometric patterns of contained pebbles set on end create a mosaic with strong contrast.

Doug Bryant created this patio, retaining wall, and seat with thick, fitted flagstones. The casual look belies his high skill level.

Slatelike stepping-stones disturb the surroundings least, blending with plantings. The ornate chairs add an element of contrast.

This elaborate patio surrounding a pool and hot tub incorporates some large boulders as well as an outdoor fireplace.

A mix of stone types makes this fire pit and benches by Todd Campbell especially colorful.

For this patio, Todd Campbell used basalt cobble risers and fringe with heavy, dry-laid sandstone platform and treads.

Everything in stonework starts with a wall (except, of course, a floor). A pier is a short wall with lots of corners. A chimney is four walls that form a tall, hollow

Drystone Walls

enclosure with some refinements inside. A lintel is a suspended wall; an arch is a suspended wall that is curved. A foundation is a wall holding up a structure. The basic unit of one stone set on another two is the nucleus of any wall.

You'll set a tall rock now and then, to break that line, and maybe two next to it to come up to its height. Some masons allow a maximum of two two-stone verticals side-by-side; the best don't. A stack of stones next to another stack, with nothing locking them together, doesn't work. *Interlocking* is the key here.

OPPOSITE: A drystone wall can be created with tightly fitted shaped stones, or simply laid with minimally shaped boulders like these.

Whether you're laying drystone or mortared work, the rule that each stone should stay where you put it, even without mortar, always applies. A rounded river rock got round by tumbling around in the water. It won't sit any better or stay where you want it to in your wall if it can teeter. The force of gravity — and the friction between stones because of that gravity — has to help you, not undo your work.

Mortar eventually disintegrates, and a poorly laid stone that depended on it will fall, along with whatever it was holding up: hence, the guideline that each rock you use should have a flat top and bottom. Now, you can take some liberties with that, so your stonework isn't simply a uniform expanse of bricklike stones. For instance, a hexagon can have a flat top and bottom and not look rectangular, because it isn't. The same goes for a parallelogram. A triangle can go next to a stone with a sloped end, so the two together create the platform for the stone above. The point is simply to use rocks that are naturally well balanced, so you don't have to glue them in place with mortar.

Another good rule in any wall-building project is to use stones as wide and long as you can. This lets you cover more vertical joints and lock more stones in place. Where you must use shorter stones in a course, cover that section with long stones in the next course up. Of course, these more massive stones take more effort to place, and you may need specialized equipment to handle them.

HANDLING LARGE STONES

THERE ARE A LOT OF WAYS to move large rocks you've found. Pry up big stones with a sturdy plank with a long digging bar, or seesaw it up with a partner. I recommend following the "two-man-rock" rule: If two men cannot lift and place a particular stone, use mechanical help. If you have access to a loader or a tractor with a bucket, you might use it to place a few big stones for accents, then fill in around them with smaller stones. You could rig a tripod over the wall, made of 2×6 beams bolted together at the top, and lift big stones with it by way of a ratchet hoist, chain hoist, or block and tackle.

For even bigger stones, you'll need to rent or buy bigger equipment. Most can be rented either with or without an operator (if you can handle the machine yourself or if you have someone else who can). The ideal machine for handling heavy stones is a swinging boom mounted on a truck, tractor, or track vehicle. This can be parked within range of the work, to lift and position the stones. A crane is usually a longer boom, often extendable with hydraulic cylinders, to reach farther from its parking spot.

Freestanding Drystone Walls

I like to start beginners on drystone work because it's a good way to learn the basic stonework principles. Interestingly, many master masons prefer to work dry, too, achieving the tight joints so much a part of our stone-working heritage. If you learn to do good drystone work, mortared stone comes easily.

So let's build a wall, a freestanding, meandering piece of landscaping that will be there for a couple of thousand years. This wall will have faces visible at front, back, top (cap), and both ends. That means you'll have to choose rocks worthy of being seen from every side, and it takes effort and planning to find those rocks.

Freestanding Drystone Construction

The classic drystone wall has face stones in both its outer surfaces, with rubble, rock chips, or big chunks of gravel inside or between them. This is called "hearting." The idea is that only the outer surfaces will be seen, so the interior can have gaps, to be filled with the hearting. (Don't use fine gravel for hearting, by the way; it'll hold dirt and moisture, which will freeze and push apart the wall.) Now, you *can* build a wall by fitting all the

Dry Stone Conservancy LEXINGTON, KY

In the mid-1990s, a 13-mile section of the historic Paris Pike Parkway between Lexington and Paris, Kentucky, was at the center of a major legal tussle.

One side of that tussle demanded the parkway's improvement — its two lanes lacked sufficient capacity to serve existing and projected travel demands, not to mention the need to address its high fatal accident rate stemming from lack of adequate shoulders, steep ditches, and various "scenic distractions." The other side fought to minimize the impact roadway realignment would have on the miles of historic drystone walls that were prominent along the corridor. These landmark limestone structures were being hauled away, buried, or ground into road rock at an alarming rate.

A solution was eventually agreed upon by the Kentucky Transportation Cabinet and the Kentucky Heritage Council: three miles of dry-laid stone walls would be rebuilt or built new to retain the character of the existing road. In each case, the rock walls would be customized to retain the style of each property owner's original fence.

The only element lacking in the ambitious plan was enough skilled masons to execute it. In 1996, the Dry Stone Conservancy was born out of the immediate need to train more masons for this massive act of preservation. The conservancy's ultimate mission includes establishing a world-class standard of craft and certification toward which all professional stone-wallers can strive, as well as creating a national center for drystone expertise.

The conservancy's instructors aim to teach their students the fundamentals of stonework by "training the body and hands in concert with the brain," says Jane Wooley, the restoration manager for the conservancy. Training personnel on the Paris Pike Parkway project were borrowed from Great Britain's Dry Stone Walling Association, and are headed up these days by training program manager and master craftsman Neil Rippingale. Workshops are structured to operate on a classic teaching formula: 10 percent showing, 20 percent telling what it is you're showing, and 70 percent guiding as the students do it themselves. Training is offered for amateurs and professionals alike — the conservancy has consulted on projects for National Park Service personnel in 35 states — and keen students hail from around the world.

internal edges tightly together, and this would make the wall extremely strong. But it would take you a big chunk of your next few months, or even years of your spare time. And no one but ants and maybe lizards would ever see all of your terrific work.

So essentially, a drystone wall is really two walls standing side by side. They slope inward toward each other, which helps the walls support each other (this is called "battering"). That inward slope isn't enough to lock everything into place, however; for that, you also need tie-stones.

Tie-stones. Set crossways to the faces, tie-stones span the width of the wall, at around mid-wall height, binding both sides. In addition to the tie-stones, some of the face stones can extend past the center of the wall, then be overlapped by others from the other face for additional strength. At the top of the wall, you'll finish with a layer of wide stones, called capstones. Like tie-stones, capstones typically span the entire width of the wall, linking the two sides for extra stability.

Tie-stones are hard to find because they go from face to face and their ends show. A stone that tapers to a point is bad; so is one that's rounded or just generally misshapen. The end of the tie-stone should look like just another face stone. It'll take some time to search out the right tie-stone, or to cut one. Capstones, too, have pretty specific traits that make them even harder to find. It's a good idea to set aside plenty of tie-stones and capstones *before* you start building your wall. As you're working, it's tempting to simply grab the best stone as you need it, but ties and caps are too important and too hard to find to be used where a smaller stone could do the job.

Stone faces. The faces of your wall stones are a matter for your own aesthetics. Some people want smooth faces; others want convoluted ones. Some insist that the faces match the slope (batter) of the wall; some don't. If you do use stones with sloping faces, make sure you place them with the face sloping toward the top of the wall, not the base of it. Besides looking sloppy, a jutting edge will catch rainwater and direct it into your wall — not a good thing.

Now, all this about flat surfaces and stone faces brings up the matter of shaping stone. You have two choices: Either search for just the right stone that fits or cut it so it does. Simply put, you must have a whole lot of extra, good stone if you want to find the right one and use it as it is. Figure on buying or collecting at least 50 percent more than you think you'll actually use. You'll also need to learn a lot about cutting stone if you plan to shape stones to fit. If

A good stone-waller will use a tie-stone in every three or four feet of length. Large capstones help anchor the wall.

capstone

tie-stone

you start out doing a lot of shaping, it will dramatically slow down the progress on your wall, and that can be frustrating. I recommend that new stoneworkers hunt for the right stone whenever possible and do little or no shaping on a drystone wall.

Designing your wall. Before you can build a wall, you need to know what you want it to do and what you want it to look like. Do you want it to serve as a boundary between you and your neighbor? Or would you like the wall to be a feature within your yard to border a path, delineate a parking space, or perhaps edge a garden? Should it be straight or have a slight curve, or will it meander among trees? Whatever you want this wall to do, make it fit the existing landscape. This may mean you want the ends of the wall to taper gradually down to the ground, so it looks almost like it has risen right from the earth. Or you may prefer the more formal effect of a straight end, either out in the open or next to a tree or a structure.

To help you visualize the finished wall, use some kind of marker (such as wooden stakes, or those little flags on stiff wire that surveyors and landscapers use) to mark where you'd like it to be. If your site isn't flat, or nearly so, pay some attention to the slope. The most natural-looking wall has a top that's level or nearly so, but that's not strictly necessary. You could step yours up a slope, build it diagonally across the slope, or curve it around a hill. You may also wind your wall between trees, but stay back a few feet from the trunks; otherwise, the growing roots will dislodge the stones.

If you get bogged down in this planning stage, don't be tempted to simply plow ahead and hope it'll all look fine when you're done. It can be worth bringing a landscape architect out to your site and paying him or her for ideas. After all, what you build here will be, for all practical purposes, permanent. (Yes, you *could* pick it up one rock at a time and move it later, but let's get it in the right spot from the beginning.)

Preparing the site. Before you start setting stones, you need to get

Avoid setting stones at a downward angle; they'll inevitably slip out.

GUIDING YOUR WORK

I'm a firm believer in standing back and sighting often as I build a wall. If it looks good, it is good. Personally, I find that using stakes and string to guide the layout isn't useful; they're a tripping hazard, and they don't help on curved walls. But if you lack confidence in your eye, go ahead and use them as you develop your technique; lots of masons do. Strings or no, though, take time to sight from several points to make sure your wall is taking the shape you want. It's easy to get tunnel vision, working close to each stone, so back off frequently.

the site ready. Dig away any soft topsoil, woods duff, or turf until you have firm subsoil, either level or in level steps. The steps can be any height; you'll just have to match that height with a stone when you get to the step.

Why can't the base simply follow the slope? To understand that, you first need to know about battering. In a freestanding wall, battering means narrowing both sides to spread the weight evenly to the base of the wall. Battering, or narrowing, as you build the freestanding wall allows each stone to sit more solidly, and helps it avoid falling off the edge if disturbed.

If your wall goes up or down a hill, the top can either step or slope. The base, however, should always step, or the wall will shift and crumble when the earth beneath it freezes and thaws. A well-laid wall will flex with this heaving, then go back where it belongs each time.

How much battering should you allow for when preparing the wall base? For a 3-foot-high wall, I like the base to be 2 feet thick with a 3-inch batter (or inward slope) as the wall goes up and an 18-inch-wide top. To create the batter, you'll simply set each course slightly in from the previous one, creating a very smooth transition from the bottom to the top of the wall.

Laying the base course. Now you're ready to start placing stones. If you're building on a hill, start at the bottom of the slope; otherwise, begin wherever you choose. Lay a base course, two stones wide, for whatever distance you feel you can handle easily. (I suggest working on about 10 feet at a time.)

With their rougher side down, set the base stones into the soil, digging out the earth to accommodate any humps, twists, or steps in them. If you lay a tall stone on one face, you can match its height with two on the other face. You want to minimize vertical joints here inside the wall as well as in its face, so it's best to overlap at the center of the wall as often as you can: it makes a better wall.

As you place the base course — all the courses, for that matter — avoid setting any rock at an outward-and-downward slope from horizontal. Such stones will sooner or later dislodge and weaken your wall. Just about every fallen stone wall had in it problem stones like this. I like to tip each face stone inward, so it tends to want to move toward its opposite stone; that makes the tie-stones harder to fit, though. The thing to remember is to avoid tipping them to the outside. Level is fine, from side to side. Level isn't that important lengthwise if you can oppose a downhill-sloping stone with another stone pushing against it.

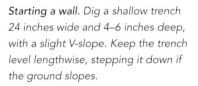

Starting a wall. Dig a shallow trench 24 inches wide and 4–6 inches deep, with a slight V-slope. Keep the trench level lengthwise, stepping it down if the ground slopes.

The base course. Place stones along the bottom of the trench in pairs, with each sloping toward the center. To leave as smooth a top surface as possible, place stones with uneven surfaces down, digging out soil as needed. If two stones are short, fill the gap with broken stones.

Stonemason Doug Bryant and his partner took advantage of oddly shaped stones to make this section of wall seem to undulate.

During the wall-building competition we hosted in 2001, Doug Bryant and his partner created a wall section that undulates, yet is stable. That section of the wall had to climb a rise and make a curve, so he chose rocks that curved up and at an angle. Some purists among the participants frowned on this as not being good walling, but it's my wife's favorite section. If you have the skill, you can stretch the rules.

Building the wall. Laying the first course of stone with a level top is pretty easy, because you can dig down as much as needed to get all of the stones even. Now, you're going to have to find just the right thicknesses to keep your courses even. Again, you can use two to match one tall one whenever necessary.

The most important thing to remember as you build your wall is to cover *each* vertical joint with a stone. That doesn't mean all of the stones have to be the same length as those below them; you can fill with a short one or bridge two joints with a long one. Don't forget to overlap each opposite face stone in the center, if you can. You need all the locking action you can get.

For strength, always use as long a stone as you can find. Short ones don't bind together well, because they have less surface area, and therefore there's not as much friction to hold them in place. About the only time I use a short stone is to fill between two that leave a gap. Set your larger stones where they fit best, even if they don't touch each other, and fill in with something small. Be sure to use a deep stone to fill an in-between

USING SHIMS

NO MATTER HOW GOOD YOU ARE, your stones won't lie entirely flat. Stones just don't do that, unless they're cut precisely. You'll have to "shim" spaces with thin chips to get out the wobble. Now remember, shims are not merely space-fillers. A wall based on shimming to replace good stonework will not last and is the mark of an amateur. Choose and place your stones carefully, then use shims only where they are really needed.

Shims take a lot of weight; use as broad and flat a chip as you can find to stabilize each stone. This will help take some of that weight from upper courses, too. A too small shim can be crushed, or it may hold up just one point of the stone, which then can crack where it's unsupported. Shims are often visible, and that's not a flaw. Just don't overdo them; select or shape your stones for closer fits instead.

Laying courses. As you lay additional courses, take care to cover the cracks between the stones in the previous layer. Try to use stones of uniform thickness (height) in each course. Where this is impossible, use two thin ones alongside a thick one for an even height.

Using tie-stones. Place a 21-inch stone every third or fourth layer (and about every 4 feet along the length of the wall) as a tie-stone. As this will be seen on both wall faces, it should have relatively straight ends. Check the slope of the batter with a level and reestablish the V-slope as necessary.

space, so it won't fall out. There's a great temptation to shove in a shallow stone that fits and hope it stays. It won't.

If you've used an average of 3- to 6-inch-thick stones, you'll go up maybe four courses before you need tie-stones. It's acceptable to have one about every 4 feet at mid-wall height. I like to put in more than that because it creates a tighter wall, but it also takes more work to find and place these large stones. They don't all have to go in at exactly the same height; fit them in where they want to go, but near that level.

If you've sloped your face stones down toward the center of the wall where the hearting is, the tie-stones will rest only on the outer edges of the wall, and that's not desirable. To support them, build up the hearting and use shims to distribute the weight evenly.

Above the tie-stones, continue as before. Check for batter in the wall often, using either a carpenter's level or a level attached to a tapered board to get the slope right. Or just stand back and eyeball the slope. At tie-stone height, your wall should be about 21 inches thick, having sloped in from both sides beginning with that 24-inch thickness. Given stone's irregularities, you've got some slack in the thickness here; just avoid glaring bulges or cavities.

Remember, you are laying this wall in manageable sections, not all in one day. Unless you're completing the last section, leave the end stepped. That way, when you start again, the work will tie in to what you've already done.

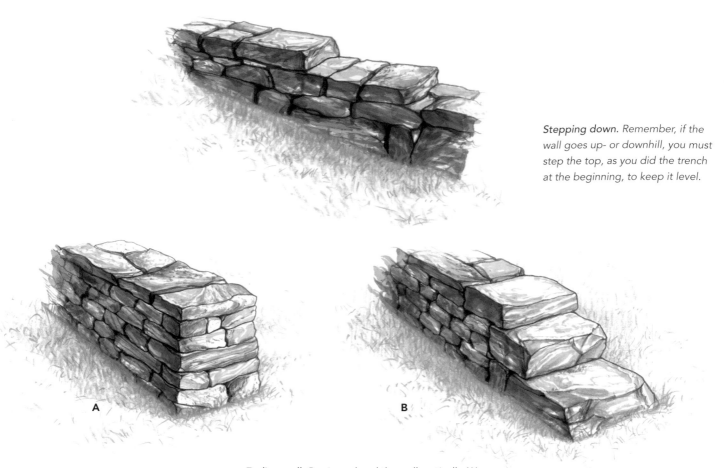

Stepping down. Remember, if the wall goes up- or downhill, you must step the top, as you did the trench at the beginning, to keep it level.

A

B

Ending well. Begin and end the wall vertically (A), or step it down to the ground (B). If the ground rises, keep the wall top level until it fades into the grade.

Finishing the ends. At a vertical wall end, use tie-stones for every other course, bottom to top. Things have a way of bumping into wall ends, and you want all the bonding you can get there for stability. If you want the wall to step down to the ground, that's okay, too. You might even want to use tapered stones so the wall slopes down instead of stepping down.

Adding the capstones. Finally, you're within a few inches of the 3-foot height. Select the style of capstones you want for both their purpose and their look. You can set them either vertically or horizontally; just keep in mind that you cannot comfortably sit or walk on vertical stones.

The best stones are as wide as the wall and as long as possible. They should all be near the same thickness, and it's best if their edges match very closely. They should also be big enough to cover as many vertical joints as possible to keep out rain, and heavy enough to stay put despite being walked on, scrambled over, bumped into, and leaned against. Horizontal capstones *must* be set for stability. Besides all this, capstones should look nice, too. (Whenever possible, I like to use mossy or lichened stones here, even if it means watering the wall in dry weather to keep the greenery alive.)

TURNING CORNERS

YOU MAY WANT A CORNER some-where along your wall. Besides allowing you to change direction and adding interest to the look of the wall, a corner acts as a "but-tress" to strengthen the wall. It also gives you the ability to provide niches for seating or a base for steps.

Here, you'll alternate, or overlap, face stones to lock the corner. Visually, you'll see the end of one stone over the side of another. As with a vertical wall end, lock this corner every way you can; it's not as strong as the straight stretches otherwise. Properly done, it's stronger.

With all these traits to look for, it's hardly surprising that good cap-stones are hard to find. If you selected plenty of caps well in advance and resisted using them during the building process, you can go ahead and finish your wall now. Don't have enough to do the job? You may be able to cut some from the stones you have left (a good opportunity to practice your cutting and shaping skills). If you don't have anywhere near enough good capstones, you could use something like cut bluestone (flagstone) to cover the wall in a smooth expanse. Just make sure it's thick and heavy enough for its weight to keep it in place.

On a sloping wall, capstones can be stepped (with overlapping ends) or sloped (which requires tapered stones). You may use triangular shapes here, with diagonal lengthwise joints, or any other matching shapes and joints. Just remember to use the largest capstones that you can.

These capstones (seen from above) were shaped specifically to turn this corner.

PATRICK MCAFEE is one of today's foremost masons. He travels the world, building and restoring works of stone and teaching stone structure. He is an expert in mortars and traditional techniques, and his work is among the finest being done today. He is a wonderful, spirited teacher, and keeps alive the continuum of stone masonry. His writings are inspiring, concise tributes to the craft and are must-reads for masons. This is his philosophy on stone:

The wind brings gray clouds across the mountain and in the air there is the smell of rain. The mind sets itself against the day ahead, the work begins, and my thoughts turn to what working with stone means to me.

When I was 18 years of age and in my third year as an apprentice, I confidently thought, this is it: I know what there is to know and I can equal most men in output. Now, nearly 40 years later, I'm still learning and am constantly surprised at how much more there is to know. Obviously there is no end to this and it is one of the aspects of stonemasonry that still excites me and the reason I like to travel, meet, and work with others. At other times I prefer to be in solitude, away from all forms of distraction, just myself and the work.

There is a physical, mental, and spiritual aspect to stonemasonry that seems to fulfill what work should be all about. The physical is in overcoming gravity and achieving balance within the work. There is the importance of pace and endurance rather than strength. The sense of well-being, physical tiredness at the end of the day, hunger and thirst, and a closeness to the elements, the sun, wind, and rain. It is quite wonderful.

Stones belong in families and each family has a different nature. To know one family does not prepare you for the next. When working by hand it is much easier to work with their individual nature rather than against it. A hammer not used for some time requires the body to readjust to its weight, length, and balance. Given time, harmony develops.

The mental aspects of the work are real and it is what struck me as a boy and reinforced math and geometry: volumes transferred to real tons and these tons had to be manually lifted. Linear, square, and cube all became reality; geometry is a never-ending fascination.

There is also the delightful muddling over practical problems, the working out of solutions: an easier way to do something, organization of a work team, a handier place to leave materials, quantities and estimating.

There is the sense of permanence in the work: It will be there a long time after we are gone. Much satisfaction is gained by being able to stand back and look at what has been done, although it is in the doing that all meaning and purpose occur for the stonemason. The age of the stone itself, incomprehensible, putting our own existence in perspective. These thoughts cross the mind of all who work with stone. There is a sense of doing something worthwhile and something good.

To pass on skills to the next generation is essential and must be done with generosity. It gives meaning to life, a river flowing through time.

As in many crafts, the point to reach in the doing of things is the one that is beyond thought. The memory of what to do is no longer in the brain but in the body itself. Much thought is put into the set-out, the organization of the work, workers, and materials, what is to be done and how it

Patrick McAfee's drystone beehive structures, one of which is a wood-fired oven.

will be done. Then the work starts, and it is mindless — well, not exactly, but pretty much so. I think this must be true of many crafts.

A love of materials and constantly learning about the nature of these materials by working with them develops an understanding of structures. It is as though you have x-ray eyes and can see through walls. This is most useful when it comes to the repair of old structures, to see how they were built. The wall, arch, vault, and dome sing a song that transcends time. We meet them as old friends everywhere in bridge, church, and castle. To work with stone requires the simplest of tools, as little at times as a hammer and a string line. Quite amazing to think that we can build a city with so little.

To do good work is to impart good spirit to what is done, and then I think something special occurs. On the mountain the clouds pass, the work at first is difficult and the body rebels against the effort, but after a while what is left is just the work.

And that elusive stone is suddenly there.

The other common dry-laid stone wall is the retaining wall, which holds back an embankment. This wall has only the one long face showing, plus ends and

Drystone Retaining Walls

capstones. It's easier to build than a freestanding wall, and when done right it can be a beautiful and functional addition to your landscape.

The principle here is to slope the retaining wall into the soil of the embankment so the two push against each other. The soil wants to keep sliding down the hill and push away the wall while the wall prevents that by pushing back harder. For a tall wall up a tall embankment, the wall will be more stable if the embankment is stepped up instead of cut in one long, smooth slope.

LEFT: A retaining wall of rounded stone is very difficult to lay. A steep batter, or slope, is required here, so each stone sits on and behind the ones below. Such a wall is necessarily a low one.

The retaining wall can be of an even thickness using the proportion of about two-thirds as thick as tall (2 feet thick for every 3 feet of height), or it can thicken as it goes up, to exert more pressure against the bank at the top, where retaining walls typically fail. A wall will fail at the top most often when the top is too light and too narrow.

I've argued with other masons about retaining walls for 50 years or so, because many walls were and still are built thick at the bottom and thin at the top like the batter of a freestanding wall. If the embankment were fluid, that would be right because there would be more pressure at the base. But it doesn't work that way, because the base of an embankment rarely moves. The upper sections, however, are subject to rain and frost and tend to erode. Erosion is what needs to be halted, so the more pressure the upper section of the wall exerts, the more it will protect the upper part of the embankment. I think the "thin-at-the-top" practice came from the freestanding shape, and the fact that it's easier to put the smaller rocks up higher than the big ones. I like to keep retaining walls evenly thick throughout, or even wider at the top than at the bottom.

Participants in a drystone walling workshop given by John Burnell build a retaining wall with sandstone rubble in Chagrin Falls, Ohio.

Building the Wall

Here's how I've built retaining walls for more than half a century, all of which are still standing, at last report. Again, let's suppose you need a 3-foot-high wall. First, dig away loose soil at the base of the embankment until you have a firm base. If your wall will go up- or downhill, step the soil at the base so each stone will be level. Some masons keep loose dirt from going through the wall by covering the raw cut of the embankment with filter fabric, but this is optional.

To get the wall to lean correctly into the embankment, start with 18 to 24 inches of thickness against the base of the bank with your first course. Leave the back edges of the stones rough, and tilt them against the cut of the slope. As you place each additional layer, step it back some to create the batter and fill in behind it with earth (tamp it down, don't just leave it loose), or use coarse gravel. Remember that a retaining wall needs more batter than a freestanding one. Here, you will want 1 foot of batter for every 3 feet of height. As with any wall, remember to avoid vertical running joints (two or more vertical joints in a row).

Placing the Capstones

Cap with the longest stones you can handle, keeping the same wall thickness you started with. Ideally, the capstones should sit a few inches above the grade. That will hold soil better, since soil tends to wash down and build up from uphill.

If you've filled behind the retaining wall with coarse gravel, cover it with filter fabric at the top to keep dirt from washing down and clogging the spaces between the rocks. (Whether or not you used filter fabric along the slope itself to control loose dirt on the embankment, you need to use it here at the top.) Otherwise, water will carry dirt with it as it percolates down and through the wall spaces. Cover the fabric at the top of the wall with just a few inches of topsoil, then plant with grass or a ground cover.

If you've filled with compacted earth at the back of the wall, some will wash into and through the wall, but it'll probably plug itself up in time, and little plants can grow in these soil-filled spaces. Here again, using filter fabric between the embankment and the stone can help keep soil leakage to a minimum. Otherwise, your beautiful stone retaining wall will get dirty with each rain, at least at first, if the clay seeps through.

Strengthening Taller Retaining Walls

If you plan a retaining wall that's higher than 3 feet, you'll need to build in buttresses or angles or curves to strengthen the wall. Buttresses are solid stone props (usually a pierlike stone column, but sometimes large single stones) built against a wall to support it.

This dry-laid sandstone retaining wall was built by Alex Rucker and Willie Lehmann in Virginia. Both the batter and the curve help hold the slope above.

Drystone Retaining Wall

A drystone retaining wall is cheaper and easier to build than a mortared wall, having no footing or mortared joints. It isn't as strong as a mortared wall, but, when built properly, can support a slope. The drystone retaining wall is more natural-looking, especially when built of aged stones rather than those freshly quarried or dug from the ground. Also, moisture seeping from the soil bank held by the wall will allow lichens and mosses to grow better on the drystone wall.

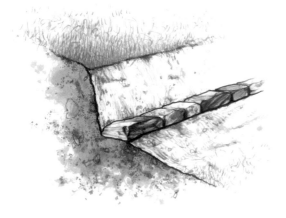

[1] Start the retaining wall with stones 12 in. deep, set against the earth bank. This layer, or course, can be any height but would typically be about 6 in. Fit the stones so they're tight at the face, and fill any spaces up against the bank with soil, tamping it firmly. This first course is a good place to use stones that have rough faces, since these can be turned down and the soil dug out to fit. Reset the layout string to keep the front faces of the stones even and straight.

[2] The second and succeeding courses of stone should be level and the faces plumb. Use increasingly deeper stones for each level, so that each stone lies on the ones below, with some of it extending onto packed soil at the back. Avoid running joints.

In keeping the face of the wall plumb, you're actually leaning the wall into the hill, holding it in place. Because each stone also slopes slightly into the bank, any frost-induced movement will be countered by gravity.

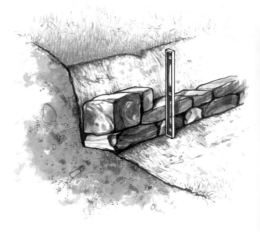

[3] The top course — the capstones — should be the full 24 in. wide (front to back) for stability. Choose these carefully and use wedges of stone to seat these solidly, because they'll get walked on. They can be any thickness, but being large, choose thin ones so you can handle the weight; 2–3 in. is about right.

The strongest buttress for a retaining wall is built into the front of the wall. This is called an exterior buttress. The buttress should be built with its stones interlocking with those of the wall. Its thickness isn't as important as its depth against the main wall; downhill movement is what we want to counteract here. Sometimes, exterior buttresses stick out so far from the wall that they get in the way. This is your opportunity to get creative, by using the niches for plantings, as part of a wall for a pool, or as little recesses for seating. These clever ideas transform the obstructions into special landscape features.

Interior buttresses are less obvious but not as strong as exterior buttresses. They are built into the bank that you're trying to hold in place. This requires carving deeper into the bank at the point where a buttress goes. Its stones are interlocked with the wall, too, but it should be stepped from deep at the bottom to wall thickness at the top. The weight of the fill pushes down on the steps and helps to hold them and the wall in place. More interior buttresses are necessary than exterior ones. I like an exterior one every 10 feet or so in a 5-foot-tall wall; for interior buttresses, I want one every 5 feet.

Elizabeth Nisos built this giant retaining wall for a retention pond in an industrial complex in Charlottesville, Virginia.

ON TWO AND A HALF ACRES in Jerusalem, two Tel Aviv–based architects, Lipa Yahalom and Dan Zur, have created a Holocaust memorial out of 15,000 cubic meters of Judaean limestone. The massive project, called the Valley of the Communities, commemorates the 5,000 communities that were destroyed by the Nazis during the Holocaust.

The memorial, which took 14 years and $15 million to build, comprises a belowground labyrinth, with connected courtyards representing each country that lost a community. The name of each community is engraved on the walls, which are arranged to correspond with the map of Europe and North Africa. Its intent is to convey the feeling of walking through a constructed ruin, a kind of open grave. As visitors move from one courtyard to the next, they're meant to feel dwarfed by the 30-foot-high walls; the feeling is not that these communities were eliminated from the earth, but rather that they were swallowed up by it.

The memorial features several courtyards like this one, each of which represents a country that lost a Jewish community in the Holocaust.

This overhead view shows the immense scale of the valley.

The 30-foot walls of the monument are constructed of Judaean limestone.

Another strengthening tactic for a tall retaining wall is a corner, or a jog, in it — ideally, a 90-degree one. That means there's a section that the embankment is pushing against at its end where it's strongest, and that's good. A few such jogs can look interesting, but too many could get busy. Again, artful plantings can help camouflage these structural additions.

Curving a retaining wall against a rounded slope is another way to strengthen it. It's normally built a little like an arch laid down on its side, holding what's behind its concave face. Building a wall that curves *away* from the slope, instead of with it, makes it stronger, but that typically isn't a natural-looking solution. Usually, adding buttresses or building a mortared wall on a footing is a better way to create a strong, attractive, and long-lasting retaining wall.

Creating Terraces

So far, we've discussed retaining walls to keep erosion down and to create usable flat spaces. With a steep slope, or for more leveling, two or more walls will result in a terraced area, or a hanging garden effect. This is how all those terraced mountain vineyards, gardens, and croplands were built in Italy, Greece, Japan, China, and Peru to enable farmers to grow produce on far-less-than-ideal terrain.

Simply put, multiple retaining walls repeat the basic goal to hold back parts of a hill with rocks. Where before we modified the natural slope into a single step, we now create multiple steps.

Planning

The natural slope will dictate the height of the walls and the lateral distance between them. The finished grade also affects the wall structure; to create flat ground, build higher walls or allow less space between them. To create a manageable slope out of the natural steep one, moderate it a little with walls.

A problem with multiple walls is getting the stone to the site. If your walls can be widely separated, and if you can level stepped areas before building, perhaps you can

NOT ALL RETAINING WALLS are created equal: each site dictates the kind of wall needed. If you want less batter, or a vertical face, your wall should be much thicker. This thicker wall will be more labor-intensive, because you will use more cubic feet of stone and/or gravel behind the face than the battered wall. The stone behind the face is an integral part of the wall and must be stable. The stones there need not be beautiful or your best ones, but they must be well laid and tied in to the face stone for a strong wall.

Step back the edges of the stones into the bank in the same way as you would have laid the face-front of a stepped wall, but use wider stones to go from the face deeper into the bank in each step up. If you don't have enough deep stones or anchor stones extending from the face to the embankment, you can double them with smaller stones here and there on any given layer. You will need to go back to using single anchors next layer up to lock them in place in the wall. Here is where you'll often set a stone endwise to the bank, with its narrow end face showing.

Go back to that good rule in any wall building: Use stones as wide and long as you can. Long stones are best to avoid vertical joints and lock the stones into each other. Long stones cover places where you had to use shorter ones in a course. This emphasizes the importance of good planning and accumulating the right stone.

get a truck or tractor up there on the terraces themselves. That will save a lot of carrying stone.

If at all possible, start with your stone supply uphill from the site. Working stones down from a pile is far easier than carrying them uphill. If the stone supply is uphill, build the lower wall first, so it won't be in the way. If the only place to locate the stone supply is at the bottom, then start with the top wall, again to create better access.

I recommend drystone for terrace walls. It is less expensive, requiring no footing or mortar and no concrete for footings. Those concrete pumping trucks are very expensive.

Preparing the Site

You may have the entire slope excavated and graded into steps first, as you would for a basic retaining wall. If you don't want the hill destroyed like this, you will want to do minimal digging. This means leveling just what you need for the foundation course and bringing in fill, perhaps topsoil, for whatever use you plan above each wall. If you intend to grow things, you'll need better earth than the subsoil the excavator will leave.

For this minimally invasive approach, pick-and-shovel about 18 inches back into the slope, following a level along the hill face, or step up or down if you choose. If the slope isn't very steep, you could use a tractor with turning plow to turn the soil for your starting course of stone. But since multiple retaining walls usually mean you have a fairly steep slope, let's be safe and do it by hand. Turning a tractor over on yourself is no fun.

Toss the excavated soil uphill for later fill and level down to firm subsoil, with a slight slope down into the hill to lean your wall into it.

Laying the Stone

Make the depth of the foundation course half your finished wall height if you're going to thicken the wall as you go up. That's 18 inches for a 3-foot-high wall that will have deeper upper stones and capstones, extending back into the hill slope. If you opt for a batter (sloped face) in the wall and want to keep it the same thickness, make the base and the wall two-thirds as thick as the height, or 2 feet thick for a 3-foot-high wall. As with any base course, bury the irregular sides of the stones in the ground, leaving flat tops for the next course.

Let me reemphasize that you can use something even as odd as a three-dimensional triangle stone, setting the inverted pyramid deep, so its flat base is up. Try to use your ugliest stones here, to avoid having to cut them for later use.

As with any retaining wall, either batter the face a little, or use

OPPOSITE: Edwin Hamilton's dry-stone terrace walls incorporate individual stones as large as 5 tons. He and his crew spent 2½ years on the job and used an estimated 2,500 tons of stone.

increasingly deeper stones to get the slope to go back into the hill. Always use the longest stones you can get for this work, and, of course, avoid running joints. Your primary need here is for strength; form follows function.

You can create a pleasing variation in the basic straight-across-the-slope wall by curving it. If there's a bulge to your hill, you'll naturally introduce a curve by following the shape of the bulge. Otherwise, you can curve the wall out by stepping it down the slope a bit, then back up, just to break the sameness of the horizontal line.

To curve the wall up into the hill, which will create a stronger wall, step up as you go back into the slope, making a concave (into the slope) shape. As with the downhill curve, you can keep the wall top level, for a taller or lower wall, or step the top, too. A series of curves, even a serpentine effect, repeated in the parallel walls above the first one, can be rhythmic and beautiful, a composition in stone. It can also make you a little dizzy if not done carefully. Judiciously placed plantings can screen parts of the walls so they don't overwhelm the eye.

Although this high retaining wall appears to be well constructed, many masons would have built it with more batter, to better retain the slope behind it.

If you decide to curve a wall, remember that the outward bulges in the wall won't be as strong as those curving back into the hill. Strengthen with stepped interior buttresses back into the slope or use long anchor stones every 3 feet or so, extending back into the soil to help hold the wall. Any shape stone will do here, as long as it has an acceptable face end, which is all you'll see in the finished wall. A convoluted shape will actually hold better, back in that hill, than a smooth one.

Of course the best bracing for any retaining wall is a series of exterior buttresses downhill to hold the face directly. These are stepped down to firm subsoil, interlocked with the wall itself. They can be quite attractive, providing angles for plantings or other features and focal points.

Finishing the Walls

Build the successive courses of the multiple walls as with a single one, mindful to tamp the fill behind the wall as you go. (I use the

Some of these stone terraces retain soil for crops; the downhill walls of the Peruvian structures are also retaining walls. A great deal of work went into getting the steep slopes level.

tamping end of a long digging bar.) I don't use gravel fill behind walls if I'm planning extensive plantings; it makes it harder to grow things, and the buildup of tillable soil is the whole reason for this exercise. Topping the subsoil fill with 6 or more inches of humus-rich topsoil, perhaps with compost mixed in, will produce better results. Fill up to capstone base level and let these stones overlap onto the soil. If you come up all the way with the fill, dirt will wash over onto the capstones and the natural buildup will be too high.

It's necessary to build steps into these multiple walls to get up through them. I like to offset these flights from each other so there's no straight-line look. It creates a little mystery if the way up is partially hidden. As with all outdoor steps in walls, each side will need additional stonework walls at right angles to the main wall to hold back the fill. Interlock these step wall stones with those of the main walls for strength, header over stretcher (a long stone alternated with another long stone the other way). These step side walls act as buttresses, too, in the main wall.

As with all dry-laid retaining walls, these will be self-draining. Although the soil will eventually plug up the spaces between the stones, they'll still let water percolate through. As part of the benefit of multiple retaining walls, they'll slow down the water on its way downhill, defeating erosion and holding it where you want it.

Elizabeth Nisos CHARLOTTESVILLE, VA

ABOVE: Elizabeth Nisos rests on the edge of the massive retaining wall she designed (see page 95).

OPPOSITE: A retaining wall Elizabeth built for a private client features many meticulously shaped stones (inset), most of which were found on the site.

"Have you ever encountered a standing chimney while walking in the woods, the house it once belonged to long decayed, vanished, only the stone remaining?" asks Virginia-based mason Elizabeth Nisos. She is passionate about masonry being the link among the existing ancient, the current, and the centuries to come. That's why masons have been "important on the planet for thousands of years," she says, and she is honored to be a point on the line of masonry history, to be a conduit of its sacred geometry.

As a child, Elizabeth would collect stones found on woodland romps and creek crawls with her dog. Later, as a teenager, she offered friends a polished stone from the collection she kept in a medicine bag around her neck: "Choose one," she would say. Today, after over two decades of building with stone, she says that often the stones choose her. Before she works, it is her custom to say a quiet prayer that she will be an instrument of "bringing stones together as they decree." She communicates a humble joy to be working with what she calls "the oldest medium on the planet," knowing that by her setting stone on stone, she is aligning them with each other for eternity.

Elizabeth began her career working for a builder who had inspired her with his descriptions of stone fireplaces and walls. For a year, Elizabeth mixed mortar,

observed, and pitched in whenever invited to. She eventually began her own business, Mountain Masonry. Over a period of years she honed her craft by working with other masons, like Toru Oba (see page 136). She works on projects as varied as stone columns at the entry to a housing development to a giant retaining wall built with enormous boulders.

"I love retaining walls!" she says with great enthusiasm, and describes a project at a 100-acre industrial development where she was able to build around the natural curvature of a pond a wall made from stone indigenous to the site, which the excavators had collected. When at all possible, she will incorporate stone taken from the land that, as she puts it, "people have been given guardianship of." The smaller-scale retaining wall she built for a residential property (above) also took advantage of stone found on the site. As she guides a visitor along the the wall, she humbly points out a carefully shaped stone (inset) that, among the hundreds used in the project, caught the attention of fellow stonemason Tomas Lipps when he came to visit.

In the center of the great room of her own house stands a massive chimney made from rocks collected from the surrounding mountainside. Elizabeth would return home from a day spent laying rock on building sites, make sure her family was fed, and have mortar mixed by 7 p.m. Night after night, she quietly, steadily laid rock until 1 a.m., until finally the chimney was completed. Whenever working in such a state of flow, her mind is serene, she says. "I'm not cognitively working; I'm an instrument, in peaceful silence." At work and at home, she lets the stones be her mentors.

CHAPTER 6

O nce you've learned the fundamentals of building
with drystone, you're ready to move on to mortar
work. You'll use many of the same principles of drystone

Mortared Walls

work — the technique is much the same. Although inexpe-

rienced masons apply mortar like glue, using small stones

that wouldn't stay stacked without it, a mortared stone

wall should be structurally sound based on the placement

of the stones. The mortar itself should add strength and

seal out moisture, but not be too prominent. After all, it's

just another aesthetic feature, and can add to or detract

from the beauty of a wall according to how carefully it's

applied.

OPPOSITE: Mortared stone-
work is stronger than drystone and seals out moisture.
It does require a footing, and
still must adhere to the principles of good craftsmanship.

MORTARED RETAINING WALLS require weep holes, which allow water to pass through the wall from the earth behind it. These can be short sections of ¾-inch black plastic pipe set at downhill grade level, every 3 feet or so, entirely through the wall. Before backfilling with soil uphill, cover with at least a foot of crushed stone (1 inch or smaller) or, better, to within about 6 inches of uphill grade level. Follow with filter fabric to keep soil from plugging the air spaces in the gravel, and then fill with topsoil for grass or other plantings. Do not use pipe that will corrode.

Before the Romans invented mortar, if stones weren't just stacked dry on each other, clay was often used to take up the spaces between them. The first mortars were basically lime and sand in varying proportions, and that continued up through the 19th century. Today we commonly mix in Portland cement to strengthen the mortar and keep it from weathering and washing out over time. Restoration work still calls for the high-lime mortars, particularly with soft stones and old brick, because the stronger Portland-based mortars tend to pull apart the softer materials as they expand and contract.

Both drystone and mortared walls are subject to the same stresses, including gravity, moisture, and soil movement from freezing and thawing. Properly built drystone can flex without damage; mortared work cannot move without cracking. The main purpose of mortar is to seal out rain and to help hold the stones in place where drystone work is not be the best building technique for that purpose. A mortared wall seals out water and roots, does not shift appreciably with temperature changes, and is much stronger than a drystone wall of equal mass. Mortared walls are also less drafty, although they are no better than drystone at keeping out the cold; stone simply isn't good insulation.

While you'll use many of the same principles to build both drystone and mortared walls, keep in mind that a mortared wall is more than a drystone wall with cement in it. It takes a lot more effort to get the base ready for building a mortared wall, and the building process itself is slower, as it takes more time to mix and apply the mortar.

Concrete Footings

Because it cannot flex, a mortared wall must sit on a firm foundation that extends below frost level. This footing, preferably of poured concrete, will be much stronger if reinforced with rebar. On a sloping site, the footing should be stepped to stay level and discourage the wall from shifting even a little bit.

The top of the footing can be as high as the surface of the ground or it can stop at 6 inches or more below it. A footing distributes the weight of the wall over a wider area, reducing the downward pressure of this weight. It is more important for the footing to be wide than deep. Building codes vary, but usually anything that requires a foundation requires a building permit.

Mixing

Before you la
stonework w
parts sand. I
or some othe
be consistent

Before m
during the t
you are wor
will want to
you need is p
standard-size
set up, in thr

I get a lo
That's a huge
ing 94 pound
army of skill
mortar befor

A heavy
use one of the
can move yo
Portland cen
you're worki
ing noise wh
than steel.

Add Water

Start with th
the wheelbar
hoe or both. T
and pour in
thin slices of
until it's wet
up, open a s
the process. I
you go. If the
mix; dry san
tar ingredien
from too dry
suggests the
water, don't

THE FORMULA FOR HAND-MIXED footing concrete is one part Portland cement, two parts sand, and three parts gravel, plus some water. How much water you'll need to add will depend entirely on how wet the sand is. The mix should retain peaks, but these should shake down flat.

moisture will condense under it and get the cement wet. And don't store Portland for more than a month. There's often enough moisture in the air to start the chemical process of setting up, which you don't want until after you mix and pour. If it gets chunks in it, don't use it.

You can buy bags of Portland cement from a concrete company, a lumberyard, or a home improvement center. You can get sand at a concrete company or a quarry. Gravel should be 1 inch or smaller (quarries call this "68"s). Crushed quarry rock generally makes stronger concrete than does rounded creek gravel.

The basic mix for concrete for the footing is one part Portland cement, two parts sand, and three parts gravel. (This is the formula for hand-mixing concrete for the footings; ready-mix will be discussed later in this chapter.) Start the mix with the sand in the wheelbarrow and then add the Portland cement, which typically comes in 1-cubic-foot sacks. Mix these ingredients dry (be sure to wear a dust mask), then add water until the mix is wet and loose. How much water you need varies a lot; a key factor is how dry or wet the sand is when you start. Add the gravel last, working it into the wet mix a little at a time.

For bigger batches, you can use a mortar box, or a cement mixer. If you use a mixer, start with a little water, particularly after the first batch, to loosen up what's left in the drum. Add the gravel next, to help scour the inside surface of the mixer; then add the sand and, finally, the cement. Add more water sparingly, until the mix flows over the mixer tines but doesn't splash out. Too wet a mix will dry with air pockets where the water was and weaken the concrete. Too dry a mix will also hold a lot of air and won't bond well. The concrete should be dry enough to hold shaped peaks when you shovel it into place, but wet enough to level out when you shake it or work it with a hoe. If water puddles up on it, it is too wet and should not be used

Pouring the footing. You'll need steel reinforcing rods (rebar), typically ½ inch thick (#4 rebar), in the footing to strengthen it. Otherwise, soft

The footing. Pour concrete at least 6 in. deep in the trench, making sure it's level. In soft ground, or where the trench goes from solid rock to soil, lay two ½-in. pieces of rebar side by side, 8 in. apart, midway in the depth of the concrete.

A rtists often define carving stone, or sculpting, as liberating the latent shapes inside. Those shapes are limited only by one's imagination and skill, the

Stone Carving

tools at hand, and the capacity of the stone itself.

Whenever and wherever stonework has been done, the masons eventually raise the craft beyond utility, beyond simple structure, to the level of art.

That's natural, given the relationship that develops between the stoneworker and his or her material. Stone is demanding, and it draws our best from us, which in turn takes the finished project past what we've done before, to new heights.

OPPOSITE: Toru Oba's stone-work is always art. Lately, he prefers sculpting stone to wall building, but even his walls, entryways, and flatwork reflect his artistry.

Bas-relief Carving

The extreme in bas-relief is cutting away stone to let complete shapes emerge. The historic stone city of Petra, in Jordan, is the ultimate example, where entire houses, temples, and public buildings were created from the solid stone of the mountain face. Unbelievable masses of stone were removed over many years to create this city, which is perhaps the most spectacular example of stoneworking of all time.

Bas-relief is most common in architectural friezes on buildings, at entryways, and on stone building panels. The Egyptians told stories in such carvings, of the exploits of rulers and heroic figures in their history.

Bas-relief carving requires a lot less stonecutting than some other projects in carving. What you're doing here is cutting away stone to let the shapes of figures or scenes stand out. The deeper you cut, the more realistic the shapes, but you can start shallow. Cutting just ¼ inch will portray a scene — a picture with just a little third dimension.

In sculptor John Sonnier's hands, stone becomes almost fluid.

If you're good at art, you can sketch the desired shapes onto the flat surface of the stone freehand. A grid is helpful for plotting the lines with reference points as they cross the grid lines. Do this on the original artwork, then on the stone itself. Another method is to project a photographic slide onto the stone surface and draw the shapes in pencil on the stone.

To begin cutting away stone, you can use a point, a bush hammer (one with multiple sharp points left by the grooves in its face), or a cutting blade, scoring and breaking out the stone to reveal the images. Angle the blade or stone point away from the penciled sketch lines so you don't break out stone across them. Don't try to use the bush hammer close to the sketched lines; it's better for removing wider expanses. You'll want a more or less even depth to the background for simple bas-relief, so don't let the cuts go too deep there (not much danger of that with the hand tools because they're so slow).

Another tool that's useful for this kind of work is the mill pick. Designed for dressing millstone surfaces, this tool has a chisel edge on both working faces; one is horizontal, the other vertical. By alternating edges, you get a cross-hatch pattern that crumbles the stone. Experiment with the weight of this tool, since one that's too light won't cut and a heavy one will give you tendonitis from overusing it. Like the bush hammer, the mill pick requires a two-handed grip.

A carved fish is a whimsical addition to this chimney in Washington.

For detailed bas-relief work, you may want to cut the background deeper, and shape arms, legs, bodies, and trees more realistically. This is more like sculpture and requires a lot more work and skill — sort of like the difference between a cartoon and a finished painting. You'll vary the depth of background cuts, and round the edges of round objects depicted. This will require a lot of fine chiseling and smoothing. You can speed this along with the grinder, but use it carefully.

A shallow, nonrealistic bas-relief carving usually has the stippled surface left by the stone point. If you've used the cutting blade extensively, you can remove its marks by dressing the surfaces with the point.

Subjects for bas-relief carving are unlimited. In ancient times, figures tended to be stylized, or even primitive in appearance. During the Middle Ages, artists strove for more realism in their work. Modern artists do a lot of symbolic stylization to get their messages across.

Mike Firkaly's "self-portrait" is carved into a stone wall sample at the Luck Stone Yard in Virginia.

PART 2

Stone Features for the Home and Landscape

Stone can form the bones of any landscaping project, from plantings and paths to pools, steps, and seats. It lends a sense of permanence because it looks as if it's always been there. And from that solid base, there are no limits to what you can do with stone; take it as far as your imagination will run.

A nything in stone that draws the eye is an accent. It could be an oversize rock high in a wall among smaller stones. It could be an unusual shape, such as a

Outdoor Stone Accents

tall vertical one in a stone tower. It could be a patio flagstone with a round hole cut in it for plantings, or a giant boulder among garden plants and flowers. The only limit is your creativity.

Accents need not be individual stones, either. A grouping at the base of an ornamental tree creates an interesting landscape feature, as does a mossy stone barely dripping water onto another, cupped one, or a flat slab cascading water onto another slab. There are really no limits to the things you can do with one or many stones to create focal points and accents.

LEFT: For this stone wall at the San Francisco Botanical Garden at Strybing Arboretum, Edwin Hamilton used limestone from a 12th-century Cistercian monastery that had been brought to San Francisco by William Randolph Hearst in the 1920s.

You don't even have to limit yourself to naturally shaped stones. Our American forebears often built up stone well boxes over their hand-dug wells and covered them with single slabs of stone, with round holes cut for the buckets. I have such a stone, with grooves worn in several places around the soft sandstone hole, where rope or chain wore them. For years I used this stone to cover a spring on our property, but have since moved it to a garden area where it can be seen and admired. The part of Arkansas this stone came from was settled about 160 years ago, which for our current age seems ancient enough for wonder.

Accent Stones

All well-done stonework is a visual pleasure, but adding one or more carefully chosen accent stones can make it truly noteworthy. For example, at our house I built stone steps around a 9-foot quarried stone that's a recycled doorsill from a factory. People start up the steps, then stop and react to that one, continuous stone. "Wow! That's all one rock?" is the typical reaction.

Accent stones occur often in nature, but you have to have the imagination to recognize them. There are, rarely, stones with right-angle cutouts in them; these look great in a wall, catching the eye every time. Early builders often placed large or otherwise noticeable stones in chimneys, house walls, bridges, or other edifices, and carved names and dates on them. I've done this, often up high if it's a big stone, to combine the message with wonder at how that big rock got up that high. It adds intrigue if the carving is just too high to make out easily.

I once consulted on the restoration of a plantation house in northern Virginia for which there was no known construction date. A scratched 1810 date on a stone in the springhouse was shown as proof of that or an earlier construction, even though the scratching was evidently recent. It hadn't weathered at all, and hadn't been done with a mason's tools. But that stone certainly serves as an accent stone today.

One of the most intriguing accent stones I've ever seen is at Machu Picchu, that repository of intrigue. At an obvious quarry site is a giant white granite stone, partially split, with holes for stone wedges still obvious. Another is a large slab, par-

A simple accent stone like this 9-foot, single-piece step inspired the design for these front steps to a porch. Unfortunately, only one of these could be found, so the rest of the steps are pieced to complement that stone.

tially worked and balanced on a stone roller evidently used to move it. In your own landscape, a split stone could be a unique addition to landscaping, showing some early mason's craft, halted in progress.

Artists, and masons who have an artistic streak, may use one quarried, polished stone among natural-shaped and -textured stones, or sometimes the reverse, with one aged surface in the midst of cut stones. Often the result is pleasing; sometimes it's jarring, but the contrast always catches and holds the eye. Remember, beauty is in the eye of the beholder, and this is as true of stonework as of anything else.

A millstone isn't in any way a natural shape, but it can evoke a whole way of life as the viewer imagines its original use. Before advanced mechanization, mills were incredibly complex workings, involving the finest woodworking, iron-working and stone-working skills. The millstone was the ultimate result of this primitive but effective technology. Invented by the Romans, it changed little over the centuries. Today, millstones are favorite accent stones. I've used them for hearthstones in fireplaces, as patio accents, and as steps.

SEEKING OUT ACCENT STONES

WHEN I TEACH STONE WORKSHOPS, I include a day of stone-gathering, which is a necessary part of learning the craft. Whether you get your stones from a stoneyard, from a former home site, from the woods, or from the roadside, you must learn to recognize usable shapes. This is no less true with accent stones. I once found a boulder in the distinctive shape of a human foot, up on a debris pile from a strip mine in Arkansas. It had definite grain, and was about 12 inches thick. I resolved to get that stone, and eventually I did. I split it into four slabs that I placed whimsically as giant footsteps in a graveled path. That was in the 1950s, and I hear it's still a conversation piece.

For structural purposes, look for stones that have a flat top and bottom. But once you've learned to shape stone, you can fudge that a lot. If a stone has character, it may be worth some cutting to get it usable for something you're building. And if it's truly intriguing, find a way to use it even if it's not structural. I recall one particular stone high on a ridge in West Virginia where I was gathering fine sandstone for the stone tower in our house. That stone looked like a miniature castle, with ramparts, steps, and mini-towers. I looked past it at first, but found myself coming back to it, imagining all sorts of places I might use it. I was by myself, though, and it weighed about 300 pounds, so I left it. I've often planned to go back up there with help and bring that stone home, to place it as a focal point in our landscaping.

Old millstones and slabs of granite serve as visually striking accents in this random stone pathway.

Raised Planting Beds

A raised bed for ornamental plantings or garden vegetables is an ideal project in stone. When made of wood, even pressure-treated timbers, these eventually decay; constructed of stone, they last virtually forever. The idea is to eliminate stooping to care for the plants, and to get them up away from trampling animals and invading weeds.

The height of the raised-bed walls is up to you, but the width is limited by your reach. You want to be able to reach all of the plants without stepping onto the soil in the bed, so it shouldn't be much wider than twice the distance you can get to comfortably (assuming that you can reach into the bed from both sides). You want to avoid making the walls too thick, because you'll need to reach over them, and the thicker they are, the less room there will be for plants. Using long but shallow stones will allow interlocking for good stability without making the wall too wide.

The simplest raised bed is of drystack, with just the topsoil dug away and the stones set on subsoil. If you prefer, the raised bed can be of mortared stone, but that means the added expense of a footing and mortar components. Mortar will allow you to build a thinner wall and will cut you some slack in stone shaping. It will settle and crack, however, unless

This squared-stone retaining wall creates a raised planting bed and also echoes the patterns seen in the house in the background.

you've gone below the frost line with the footing and sealed all the joints tightly. With well-laid drystone, about all you'll have to worry about is dislodging the capstones, which will be narrower than those in a more substantial wall.

I like to use crushed stone or gravel in the base of a raised bed to drain the soil properly. Filter fabric on top of this will keep the garden soil from plugging the gravel. Then fill the bed with good topsoil or a mix of topsoil and compost, chopped leaves, or other organic matter.

Few people stop with building just one raised bed. If you have the room, set them up in rows or any other pattern you like. It's also not necessary to make them rectangular. You can curve them or even make a simple maze of them. As long as they're not too deep to reach into comfortably, the possibilities for raised beds are endless.

A large boulder with a shallow carved pool anchors the center of this garden made up of granite-edged vegetable beds.

WONDERFUL WALL ACCENTS

WE WERE RESTORING a stone miller's house on the Hardware River in Virginia several years ago, and part of the work was stabilizing a retaining wall upslope behind it. There was one rock there, more than 10 feet long and about 3 feet tall and deep, that stood perfectly in place as the foundation stone of the wall. On reflection, I'm almost certain that stone was there to begin with and the builder used it as the starting point for the wall. You can create a similar effect by including a large boulder in your own wall project. Almost any shape will do, but of course it must be bedded solidly. If the face of this stone isn't flat, it hardly matters. The effect is one of the boulder's having been there all along and the wall fitted to it.

The difficult part, aside from finding such a stone, is of course moving it. You may need an earthmoving contractor to help. He'll have a track loader to load the big rock and a dump truck to haul it. You may need him to move it around and into place, too. Keep in mind that heavy equipment almost always leaves scars on stones. I like to be there to direct this activity, to try to keep scrapes and gouges on the bottoms or back sides of these accent stones. Over time, these will wear off, but scarred stones are one of my pet peeves.

If you set a big boulder in a wall and the stone is rounded or protrudes, this is an ideal place to plant a sedum, which is a sort of creeping, mosslike plant. It'll take hold if the surface of the big stone is rough, like granite, or has pockets and a lot of texture in it. I also like ferns planted at the base of such stones. Part of the appeal in their size is the way plants complement them.

Any large stone will become an accent, if for no other reason than wonder at how you got it into place. I've put long stones in walls, set in big, odd shapes to break up the monotony of any and all stonework, and placed random big stones way up high where you'd expect to see only small, easier-to-handle ones.

But a stone need not be large to draw the eye. While building one of the limestone chimneys for Bill Chatfield's restored log house in Kentucky, I came upon a perfectly round but flattened stone, like a big doughnut without a hole. I put it high on the chimney, with Bill's initials and the date carved in. Today, with aging, the chimney looks like the 1980 construction date might just as well have been a century or two earlier.

Kevin Fife NORTHFIELD, NH

ABOVE: Kevin Fife uses an old time "stone ax" of metal blades on edge (similar to a bush chisel) to flatten and texturize blocks of granite that will be used for the base of post-and-beam building uprights.

ABOVE RIGHT: Kevin Fife rebuilt this 200-year-old wall from the ground up by meticulously replacing the original fallen stones.

OPPOSITE: Kevin Fife reconstructed the stone retaining wall in this cemetery in New Durham, New Hampshire, using the original hand-cut granite pieces on-site.

Stopping off to enjoy a close look at the stone foundation of an old New England mill — one that New Hampshire native Kevin Fife might even have visited as a child accompanying his father, who checked water level and flow of old area milldams for the New Hampshire Environmental Services — one word comes to the master stonemason's mind: *beautiful.* Because people feel the same way about his work, he is honored today by invitations to represent both his craft and his state at such venerable gatherings as the Lowell Folk Festival in Lowell, Massachusetts, and the international Smithsonian Folklife Festival.

"If you ask ten masons to build the same wall, it will look different every time," Kevin says. His walls take their influence from the cut-granite boundary walls that once divided New Hampshire's pastures, as well as the work he saw in the Shaker Village of his hometown Canterbury, New Hampshire, which in recent years he had the opportunity to fully restore, completely dismantling and rebuilding a major portion of the cemetery's stone walls.

A high school summer job assisting the mason who maintained and mended the buildings and cobblestone walkways of Concord's prestigious St. Paul's School led to

his study of environmental conservation and art at the University of New Hampshire. Kevin built his first wall, while working in landscape construction, out of quarried Vermont flat stone, "which," he says, "*has* to be level to look good." A boss showed him how to break joints and some filler basics, and from then on it was trial and error.

Kevin differs from other masons in that he likes to use a lot of big boulders, especially in the base. But in drystone work he doesn't generally advocate bending the traditional rules. He recommends laying rock in its naturally horizontal state to ensure its strength in the construction. If it's all tied together well, he says, gravity and friction "are going to hold it . . . but horrendous work will be on the ground the next year." He wants more people to do good stonework, and to that end he teaches occasional workshops to anyone eager to learn the craft.

"Stone is a natural thing, a natural element in landscape; a stonemason is just creating forms with it," he tells participants.

These days Kevin relishes the opportunity to restore historic New England stone structures, from 18th-century meetinghouses to village walls, from old barn foundations to cemeteries. He has a buddy in the demolition business who luckily has been a source for hundreds of tons of old granite foundation stone over the years, but whenever possible Kevin will use the very stone to repair a structure that it was originally part of.

Of the walls he constructs from scratch — his Bobcat's hydraulic thumb clamping down on boulders that he'll place over a base of crushed stone (to combat damage from the deep New England frost) before carefully adjusting everything by hand — he admits he likes to go back after a few years to check on them. He is curious to see whether moss and lichen are growing on them, if each wall looks like it has always been there. His greatest joy is finding that his stone wall has blended into everything surrounding it, unbudged.

Entryways

Entryways are often attractive accents in stone. An entryway can be as simple as two standing stones, preferably with some wall leading away from each of them. Generally, these are set either deep in the ground (about a fourth of their height) or into concrete, to get more height. Monolithic entryway stones, which are ideal for flanking a driveway, can be any shape, even mostly round, but there should be a fairly vertical face to the entry. Unless you're installing a gate, the stones serve mainly as visual barriers, and they need not be higher than 4 feet or so. There's a psychological perception of enclosure with even a low wall, and the entry needn't be much taller than that wall.

A Double-column Entryway

After single stones, plain pillars are the easiest type of stone entryway. Again, these can be any shape, but the simplest is a square structure, mortared, on a footing. (Entryways are usually best in mortared stone, because somebody will eventually bump them with something large.)

If you're building 3-foot-wide, 6-foot-tall columns, dig and pour 4-foot-square footings below the frost line. I like to set a hefty piece of steel rebar — say, ¾ inch wide and about 3 feet long — into the center of each footing to reinforce the column. Build around the steel as you would any other column or pier, taking special care with the many corners.

These simple stone pillars mark the entry to a beach path.

Building a column requires a great deal of "eyeballing," as well as the use of plumb bobs or other level gauges, to keep things straight. Another thing to watch for is the tendency for a square column to twist as it rises. I like to build both entryway columns at once, and sight across often to keep them in line. Check often for square, too. If you've set that steel bar plumb and in the middle, that becomes the basis for keeping you in line and in square.

If you plan to install gates, you can set the pintles for the hinges in the mortar between the stones as you lay the stone instead of in drilled holes. I use flattened pintles, either zigzagged or barbed, to hold better in the mortar. Be sure to set these plumb or the gate will swing when you don't want it to.

It's traditional to build in a bead near the top of the entry column. For a 3-foot-square column, a 3- to 4-inch-high bead can extend out 2 or 3 inches. Anchor this with another 6 inches or so of stone, back on the vertical plane, to top off the column. Always mortar the top tight to keep water from getting inside it.

Variations on this double-pier entryway are endless. A driveway entry is usually off a perpendicular road, so you must leave space for the turning vehicles. Often, the wall or fence that encloses the property will bend inward at an angle to the entryway itself. A popular design for an entryway is a pair of taller columns close to the driveway with a stone wall extending back, sloped downward, to a lower set of columns. This section of wall can be curved, parallel to the road, or angled from it. Build the wall at the same time as the columns to lock them together. A cold joint here will almost always separate.

A tall, wide archway is sometimes used as an entryway, but this is something of a hazard. You never know when you or some future owner will want to bring a vehicle through there that's too high or too wide for what you've built, and the results could be disastrous. The same caution applies to when the stone piers are linked above truck height with a wood or metal crosspiece.

MOUNTING GATES ONTO STONES

IF YOU DO MOUNT A GATE, perhaps a wrought-iron one or a double gate if it spans a driveway, you'll have to drill holes for mounting hardware. Masonry drill bits in heavy-duty electric drills will do this, but it's not quick. Even the softest stone takes awhile to drill. If you go at the stones with a jackhammer, you might shatter them. Given time, you can use a handheld star drill and hit it repeatedly with a hammer. That's the way stonecutters worked until power tools became common.

Anchor bolts into the holes with lead or plastic anchors, which spread when tightened and hold the bolts in place. Early masons drove in iron pintles, which are serrated corner pins bent up vertically to hold hinges. Once you get some metal in there tight, you can attach things like hinges and latches to it.

Archways and Moon Gates

Garden path gateways are basically like driveway entries, except they usually are smaller. Here, if you don't use heavy machinery that might bump it, you can do an attractive archway. Either build the stone wall high on either side of it, incorporating the arch, or build the arch up off the wall ends at either side. Make the arch substantial enough to hold itself together. I like a foot of thickness and for the arch itself to be around 18 inches tall for a 3-foot-wide opening. A semicircle is among the strongest arch styles and probably the most attractive shape for such an arch.

A moon gate is an extended form of the arch, with a base that continues the overhead semicircle. These are no more difficult to build than the arch. A moon gate is almost always set as an opening in a wall, so the curved bottom portion is just a variation of the vertical wall end you'd do for any other opening. If the wall is tall enough, the moon gate becomes a round hole in the wall. If it's a relatively low wall, usually halfway up the circle, the arch rises out of it as it would normally.

Doug Bryant's stone archway, very near the San Andreas fault, is mortared and reinforced with steel. The keystone is Portuguese blue marble.

Any overhead stonework should have enough mass and be laid well enough to stay in place even with the occasional bump. Don't expect gravity to give you much slack here. You can step up the height of the wall just to accommodate the arch, but that tends to look contrived. One treatment I like is to build a high wall to strengthen the arch, but leave small round, arched, or square window openings in the wall to see through.

Grottoes

A grotto, whether enhanced-natural or entirely man-made, is an advanced project, but among stonemasons it's the favorite fantasy in stone. There is often falling water inside, or at least a pool. Grottoes can be sited at a natural rock outcropping. Today, most grottoes are typically built into stone retaining walls, creating sheltered recesses that hint of mysterious depths. When accented by plantings, these partly screened openings become even more inviting.

Any recess in a retaining wall requires digging back into the slope, then essentially cornering the wall back. For a recessed seat, for instance, the wall is simply stepped back squarely, with the stones all the way to the caps, then following the seat shape back out to the wall face. A grotto is usually rounded, so the front corners, while perhaps 90 degrees, give way to a curved back wall. This wall, including the corners, is corbelled out (stepped a few inches at a time) to close the recess in a dome shape. It's actually a three-dimensional arch supporting itself. The sides of the grotto can be giant, sloped-in stones that look as if they might have fallen into that shape or the grotto can be capped with one or two gigantic flat flagstones. (If you use two, both must extend across the entire top.) Whatever top is built, if any, it should be safe and blend with the landscape around it, which may mean building up the grade above.

A simple grotto usually has an accent stone inside: a stalagmite-looking focal point or any unusual shape. Sometimes there is a ledge for sitting. Grottoes are always cool, and there is the feel of a delightfully primitive cave. Add water, preferably trickling from above, and the effect becomes magic. It's a simple matter to bury a pipe behind the retaining wall, directing the flow over a ledge up high inside the recess, through a small hole in the roof itself or through the crack between two capstones. A plastic liner or concrete basin can waterproof the pool inside, and a quiet submersible pump can be placed right in the water.

Sometimes the water drops from up high right onto the accent stone or into the pool in the center. This lets you move around behind the falling water, and the effect is even more three-dimensional. When the water falls naturally down the rear wall, it effectively cuts off space back there, unless you want to get wet. This is where a concrete-lined pool to collect the water is good instead of a plastic liner, since it won't get damaged. A couple of mossy stones will camouflage the concrete.

Grottoes can look like natural breakdowns of stone, with heavy slabs cantilevered from each side. There can be one or more slabs leaning inward to form a tepee-like opening. The basic idea is to form a shadowed retreat that is safe to enter, partially hidden, and inviting. I prefer the pleasant chaos of seemingly random stones, giving the distinct appearance of natural placement. Others like finely placed stones, resembling an ancient dwelling or cache of some kind.

Of course, the wall itself must be high enough to contain the grotto. There are limits in height for drystone retaining walls, and indeed they must be thicker and heavier the higher they go. And a wall shouldn't

Suzanne and Ron Dirsmith created this famed grotto at Hugh Hefner's estate.

A grotto can be a cool, welcoming spot in summer. Be aware, however, that it can also offer shelter for wildlife.

suddenly rise up to accommodate the grotto, or you lose the effect. An entrance height of about 4 feet is enough, so a wall at least 6 feet tall would be proportionate. If the slope goes on up behind, place some large lichened or mossy stones above, with plantings, to suggest that the hill is all natural stone.

A grotto is also an ideal place to originate a garden stream. Springs often start in openings among stones against a hill, so this can be the beginning location for your watercourse. It simply means locating the recirculating pump in the pool at the other, lower end of the stream instead of in the grotto itself. This is often better, because there's no pump noise, however slight, in the recess itself.

Some grottoes are nothing more than a jumble of large stones up against a steep slope, with relatively big spaces between them to suggest depths. You wouldn't get inside something this simple, but again, there's room for some imagination here. And accent stones are all about imagination.

WATCH OUT FOR WILDLIFE

AS WITH ANY DRYSTONE work, the crevices in the grotto will be cool, inviting places for other creatures besides you and your guests. Always keep your eyes out for snakes, wasps, and spiders inside. Nobody ever mentions these denizens, but they do exist, and they love sheltered places in stone; that's just a fact of life. Frequent occupation by humans will help scare away creatures, but it's still a good idea to look around inside with a light before your garden party arrives.

What should you do if you find unwanted residents? Spiders and wasps can be sucked into a shop vacuum. Snakes require, first of all, someone who's not afraid of them. He or she can pull the snake out with a rake and then relocate it far away. Trouble is, by the time you spot the snake, your grotto has become its home, and the snake will likely return. Frogs, too, will find your grotto, and you may well want to keep them. They do multiply, however. One took up residence in the stones behind the recessed pool I was building in a retaining wall three years ago. It let me know it was there each time I started work, and that it was quite happy with the home I was providing for it. The owners tell me that it (or its progeny) continues to occupy that space. Everybody's happy with the arrangement.

OPPOSITE: Although some grottoes are not much more than a pile of rocks at the start of a watercourse, this one has been carefully constructed with large slabs of stone.

Obelisks and Other Standing Stones

A complete departure from the natural look in focal points is the obelisk, or spire. This consists of a single tall standing stone, and it's always a pleasant discovery in landscaping. Obelisks have a long history as prehistoric landmarks, boundary markers, single surviving gateposts, and supporting columns for long-departed slabs spanning above, as at Stonehenge. Tall shafts of stone have a real presence and can be attractive garden accents.

Rebecca Wellen has such a stone spire among the junipers at her home in Santa Fe, New Mexico. It's of the red sandstone of the region, matching the finely detailed stone and wood entryway and the giant boulders of a fountain and pool. As a guest there, I came upon the spire on an early-morning walk and felt I had encountered an old friend. Of course, a spire should have some height for effect. A 2-foot standing stone doesn't look like a spire because it isn't one. Rebecca's looks to be about 14 feet tall, and its effect includes wonder at how it got there. That's also part of the appeal of giant boulders and slabs in any stonework.

Three stone monoliths prominently mark the entry to this house.

A spire stone is typically slung from and set with a crane or boom of some kind, which can be used to balance it properly and hold it from the top while backfilling. The important thing here is to sink the stone into the ground far enough to stay upright. An 8-foot shaft should be buried 2 to 3 additional feet in the ground, which should be tamped well when backfilled.

If you set the shaft of your spire into concrete, the stone doesn't need to be as deep — just below the frost line is enough — but make the base 1 foot wider than the shaft all around, or it might tip if something crashes into it. Cover the concrete base with some topsoil so you can plant around the base of the stone. I suggest low-growing plants or a lightweight vine, such as a clematis, which should only partially obscure it. I'd avoid heavy vines like honeysuckle and wisteria because they don't know when to quit. Or just leave the stone bare; it will elicit enough awe on its own.

Naturally, the idea of a standing stone triggers images of groupings, and the most famous is Stonehenge, on the Salisbury Plain in England. This was probably a covered structure originally, but it's typical of stone circles in ancient Britain and other places the world over. Circle stones need not have the height of the single spire but can be quite impressive with 4- to 5-foot stones. They actually look better the more varied they are in shape, as long as they stand, which gives viewers the certainty that they were placed by hand and, of course, gives rise to speculations of mysterious origins.

An aisle of standing stones is also intriguing. It suggests an ancient pathway bordered by these vestigial "boundaries." If you curve such a double row of stones off out of sight around plantings or some natural feature, or even over a drop in the level of the land, folks will want to follow them. End with a pool, a really big boulder, stone seats, or any other destination you can imagine — or maybe have no destination at all.

Ruins

Ruins fascinate people. Imaginations go wild at the sight of placed stones, which suggest ancient buildings or worship sites. The evidence of human craft is the essen-

A simple stone or two can bring a touch of the natural world back into a tidy suburban yard.

tial element. Could someone have *lived* here, long before us? Could this crumbling wall have housed pagan priests? Was this a prehistoric gathering place, now encroached upon by suburbia?

I recall the ruined stone walls of Invergarry Castle, the seat of my ancestors in Scotland. It's perched on the Rock of the Raven, from which comes our surname. The castle was burned in 1746, after its McDonnell clan harbored Prince Charlie Stuart. The great fireplaces yawn, the empty beam sockets wait, the stair tower has collapsed. Loch Oich laps at the base of the Rock, and the bloody legacy of the place broods heavy. The arrow loopholes in the 4-foot-thick walls recall the interclan wars, the ongoing battles with the English, violence. But it is the garden walls, with the ancient wrought-iron gates, that hold me. Large trees grow right out of the wall tops, with roots going firmly down through standing stones to anchorage in soil. Lichens grow like beards everywhere, and the incessant rain drips.

We know much of the history of this ruin, but it still exerts a powerful spell of mystery. A contemporary ruin in a garden or in the woods can have some of the same effect. Those who experience it can imagine their own history.

The Minder Ruin Garden at Chanticleer in Wayne, Pennsylvania, was created from the remains of a razed stone house on the property.

Building Your Own Ruin

A ruin can be anything: a wall with stones tumbled at the end; a circular partial tower just a few feet tall; or a wall section with a doorway or window in it. Stones placed at a stream bank suggest where there once might have been a covered bridge or the remains of a gristmill. Perhaps a stone mouth in a hillside points to an ancient spring.

The only requirement for a ruin is aged stone, taken off the top of the ground, with no new cuts or faces. It should suggest a former use, but that use need not be specified. Put together enough stones to make it obvious that some builder at some time built this, and your ruin has come into existence. How far you go with it is up to you, your art, and your imagination. I would say less is more, within reason. A nearly complete ruin would take more stone, more labor, and leave less to the imagination.

A simply built ruin that would enhance any landscaping project would be a wall of stone that looks like a remnant, with fallen stones around it to suggest that perhaps it was originally part of a structure. But let's take it up higher: build it high enough to include a window. That definitely places it as a structure, of one sort or another. If the window frames a particularly attractive part of the garden or house, or a tree or waterfall, it will be an irresistible spot. We like to look through openings of all kinds. Windows have two functions: to let light in and to allow seeing out. This ruin affords another: an opening to the imagination.

Plantings will help obscure the wall itself and add to the appearance of age. If you can find mossy stones, this is the place to use them. Other stones in your landscaping will appear to have been looted from this ruin sometime in the past. When asked the nature or origin of such a ruin, the best reply is "Who knows?" with a shrug, or maybe "It looks like it's always been there," or "What do you think it could have been?"

Make your ruin solid and safe, because children will find climbing on it irresistible. Adults, too, will want to lean on the windowsill and imagine scenes from bygone years. You may well want to mortar this work just for the added stability. If you do, water the deeply recessed joints often, and mosses and lichen will eventually take hold there, just from spores borne on the wind, to age them appropriately.

Cairns

Stone cairns are intriguing structures. They hint of ancient altars, or of landmarks, old property corners, or commemorative markers telling of happenings in time out of mind.

A cairn is simply a pile of stones fitted so it stands as obviously man-made and purposeful. There are really no rules for this structure, although following the basics will result in a more impressive one. A 5- or 6-foot-tall cairn makes more of an impression than a low mound that's evidently fallen down from poor construction.

Build a cairn anywhere; it'll be a focal point no matter where it is. Any dimension will do, as long as there's some height, but let's say we'll build a cone 3 feet in diameter at its base and 6 feet high. Since this is a solid structure, it's best to slope each stone inward, against its opposite, or one in between. At the base, and wherever the outside stones don't fit together tight with whatever's inside or opposite, fill with chips and chunks of stone. This hearting is the same as in a drystack wall, providing blocking for stones that want to slide inward with temperature changes. The sloping will keep them from sliding outward.

A homeowner in Delaware created this simple cairn with stones left over from a project in his backyard.

Setting the Stones

Dig away topsoil and set the first course with that inward slope. I like to start with one or more big stones, even boulders. Nothing makes any stone structure look more fitting than for it to appear as if it's been built around the rock that was there from the beginning. Even though few ancient cairns were carefully fitted on their outsides, give this, as all your stonework, your best effort. Search out or shape each exterior stone for an even curve, and span vertical joints. Use irregular stones if they can be laid soundly (flat tops and bottoms), and build with horizontal layers.

Successive courses should have a rake, or inward taper, as you go up. Tapering from the 3-foot base to about 18 inches at the 6-foot top is proportional, so you can figure the batter at 1½ inches per vertical foot. Cut a tapered board if you wish, using a level to get plumb. I do it by eye, as did the ancient builders (we suppose).

There's a temptation to build a cairn with any rock that fits, but make sure it'll stay put. Don't allow any of your stonework to fall down, or you'll miss out on the craft's prime characteristic: permanence.

I like to place a cairn around a turning in a path, or in a sudden opening in the trees. Its unexpectedness is part of its mystique.

The question always is "What is it, and what's it doing here?"

The answer always is "Intriguing you."

CHAPTER 10

R eady to tackle some outdoor stonework? Here are a few starter projects, although you may well dream up some others on your own. Those listed

Backyard Projects

here are not meant to be simply blueprints for your work; they should spark more ideas of your own. Try variations on these or start from scratch, using your imagination as your compass. The principles of stonework in general are meant to guide — not limit — you in the basics of solid, safe, long-lasting work. Try anything you like, as long as it stands and lasts. Some of these suggestions may help you get started.

OPPOSITE: Large slabs of stone can be used in a variety of ways — a patio, steps, a bench — and have a massive impact on the design of a landscape.

seat, set the leg stones so their tops are 12 inches above the ground. For extra stability, angle the legs: instead of placing them at right angles to the length of the slab, slope them in about 4 inches at the back. This angle will keep the seat from tipping over sideways, because each leg braces the other, linked by the friction with the slab.

Dig the legs into the ground and bed them in gravel or crushed stone so they won't move, or set the legs in concrete. Use a mix of one part Portland cement, two parts sand, and three parts gravel, plus some water, to fill with around the legs. Be sure the slab is securely set while the concrete is still soft, or it might set up crooked and leave a wobbly seat. Leave the level of the concrete around the legs an inch or two below the surface, so grass can grow in soil over it.

Try not to shim a stone seat. Children climbing on it, big people plopping down on it, and things piled on it will dislodge a small chip. Reset one or both legs as necessary for a solid fit, or shape to get four widely spaced points of contact. You do not want that seat, which can weigh a quarter of a ton, to move — or worse, to fall on someone.

A simple stone bench can provide a meditative resting spot in the garden.

he will have memorized 10 to 20 stones at any given time. "Choosing a stone for a space is predominantly by sight, but also by feel," he says. "When my fingers become abraded, or the weather turns cold and I have to wear gloves, my progress is always slower because my ability to feel the shape of the stone is reduced."

Although Andrew is happy to build simple, traditional Yorkshire-style walls, he also likes to introduce his clients to the many creative possibilities inherent in building with stone. For instance, one client wanted his large sheepdog to be able to keep deer at bay by roaming beyond the confines of the 4-foot-high stone walls Andrew had built. To accommodate the situation, he incorporated a "lunky hole," a low passage built into the base of a wall, traditionally designed to create easy passage for grazing sheep.

For another client with three young boys, he noticed that the location of the wall he was building would cut off the boys' shortcut to where they caught the school bus every day. Noting the boys' chronic tardiness and observing their daily sprints across the lawn, he built a stile — individual slabs of stone that penetrate into the core of a wall on both sides, spaced like steps — which was traditionally built to allow a shepherd to cross over a wall while keeping the sheep enclosed.

Creative problem-solving and innovative applications for traditional drystone walls is a challenge that Andrew revels in. Working in the United States has had a powerful impact on the level of creativity and artistry that he brings to his work. When asked about this, he says, "Because so much of the land in England is agricultural, the primary reason for building walls is fencing — confining livestock and establishing boundary lines. Here in the States there are greater opportunities for being creative and treating stone and the landscape as artworks."

Choosing a stone for a space is predominantly by sight, but also by feel.

A Built-in Stone Seat

My favorite stone seat is one recessed into a retaining wall. Ideally, the seat should be a single large slab that's about 4 inches thick. Two stones with a joint here will probably settle, leaving an uncomfortable ridge in the seat, although you can adjust this later. Another drawback is that the joint will wick moisture up, long after the stone surface of the seat is dry after rain. That can make the seat unpleasant to sit on, as well as leave clay stains on your clothes. It's worth seeking out one special stone for the seat here.

When you excavate a slope for a wall, cut out an area about 18 inches deeper and about 2 feet wider than you want the seat to be. Let's say you want a seat that's 20 inches wide by 4 feet long. In this case, you need to dig back into the bank about 3 feet and about 6 feet along it before you begin the retaining wall in this section. Leave the subsoil in this rectangle about 12 inches high, to support the seat base. (With the 12-inch base topped by a 4-inch slab, the seat height will be a comfortable 16 inches.) Now build the first few courses of the wall as you would any retaining wall, up to that 12-inch height. Fill or compact as necessary to get the grade back there even with the tops of the wall course stones.

Now, if you're lucky enough to have a 6-foot-long by 3-foot-wide slab, you can lay it on the raised soil to serve as the seat, then build the walls and back on its edges. Otherwise, begin the side and back walls on the soil base. Using stones that have smooth faces (so they won't be uncomfortable to lean against), build the sides and back about 12 inches thick, making 90-degree corners by overlapping stones from the front of the retaining wall and the sides of the cut-out area. Take the side walls for the seat back a total of 30 inches, overlapping the side-wall stones with those of the 12-inch-thick back wall at the inside corners. In our example, that'll leave you with a rectangular space that's 18 inches deep and 48 inches wide.

Now you need to place the seat stone, if you haven't already done so. To fit inside the already walled-in niche, you want a smooth, flat stone that's 4 feet long and 20 inches wide (2 inches will overhang the base at the front). Get plenty of help to set this stone, which can weigh 300 to 400 pounds. Two strong people *can* set it, but it'll be a finger-smasher trying to edge it back into place. Here's where it can be handy to rig a tripod, with a ratchet hoist from the peak. Shorten the back leg so it sits up on the slope above and space the two front legs wide enough so the stone will go between them when it gets high enough to go onto that 12-inch-high shelf. Lift it carefully, with straps around two places to balance it hooked into the hoist hook. Keep your feet, and anything else you want to retain, out from under it as you lift the slab.

OPPOSITE: This seat is built into a fieldstone retaining wall that surrounds the deck of a swimming pool near Charlottesville, Virginia.

The stone probably won't sit solid the first time you set it in place. If it's far off, lift it again and use gravel fill to bring up the low places, then reset it. Ideally, the slab should tilt forward about ½ inch so water runs off. Once the stone sits the way you want it, use a long digging bar to raise the slab to remove the straps, and to lift it so you can get gravel under it to fine-tune how it sits. Last, if there are sharp corners, use a cutting wheel at an angle to round off the edges.

Grass underfoot is nice in this seating area, because it'll become a favorite spot. Round creek gravel can work too, but it rolls around and almost always will get invaded by grass. At the least, dirt, dust, leaves, and twigs will eventually fill it in, or it'll sink into the ground. You can underlay gravel with 6-mil black sheet plastic to keep grass and weeds from coming up through it, but debris will still build up there. My favorite footing material in a heavily used seating area is flagstone, ideally of the same kind of stone you used for the wall and seat. Start laying it up against the walls with about a 1-inch joint, or start a foot or so away from the wall to leave space for flowers, ground covers, or dwarf shrubs. Don't plant large shrubs or trees here, because the roots will buckle the flagstone or the wall.

A stone seat can even be built into the surrounding hillside. Growing fragrant or textural plants around the bench would provide added enjoyment for seated guests.

A Cantilevered Stone Seat

If you're fortunate enough to have a steep slope on your land, the possibilities for creative stonework multiply. Waterfalls, jumbled boulders, steps, inviting recesses in stone — all these and many others are easier and more natural on an incline.

If there's any kind of view, either a long one or close up, you need a seat to better enjoy it. A seat on that slope gives you perspective and opens up more to the eye. One of my favorites is a simple slab set so it projects from the face of the hill, creating a horizontal, inviting place to rest. Such a seat can be reached from above, down steps, or from below, up steps. It could be at the end of a path alongside that's cut into the shape of the hill — a destination.

This bench shows an artful combination of large slabs, lichened boulders, and stacked pieces of slate.

Choosing and setting the stone. Find a smooth slab of stone, from 4 to 6 inches thick and maybe 3 feet wide so two can share it. You'll need about 4 feet of length at least, so the stone can cantilever out from its anchor. A smooth creek stone would be nice here, but a sandstone or limestone piece of stratum from the woods would look more natural. Smooth any sharp corners by sweeping with the grinder blade.

Positioning such a stone will require machinery, or if you can get it delivered uphill, you can work it down into position with a long digging bar. You'll need to set a supporting stone or stones below it, much like a section of retaining-wall foundation course. Keep the tops of the stones level and set them solidly into firm subsoil. Dig a level place back into the hill, even with the tops of these stones so two-thirds of the slab's length will rest solidly.

Now set the stone with the other one-third out over the supporting stones. If you haven't been able to start with the stone uphill, a crane would be efficient here to set the big stone. Or you might bring the rock up in a track loader bucket. Wheeled conveyances tip too easily on steep places.

If you've started from above, use your digging bar to bring the stone down, perhaps utilizing a round section of firewood as a roller where possible. Be careful, once you have it close, not to dislodge your support stones. It's good to have help here, with one bar prying the front of the slab up while the other nudges it onto those stones. Keep on until you have it set, with that one-third of its length out in space.

Finishing the Seat

Now, you have two basic options for holding down the back of the slab. If it's long enough, just cover it with soil, re-creating the natural slope you cut away; then plant with grass or some other soil-holding cover. If the stone is short, place a heavy stone on top of it, maybe to form a sort of seat back. This stone will also serve to hold the soil behind it, so get a thick one and set it solidly.

Make your steps or path to this stone seat come from the side, at or below the level of the seat. It will be a welcome resting place after a climb or a walk.

STONE TABLES

IF YOU LIKE THE IDEA of a stone seat, you may also enjoy making stone tables. They work well with wrought-iron, teak, or redwood chairs, and they can be any shape. The one requirement is that the top be one piece of stone. Here's where you might want to use an irregular-shaped quarried stone slab, maybe one that is polished on top.

Obviously, a stone table needs solid support. That could be a round, built-up

pedestal of mortared stone set on a footing below the frost line, so it won't settle and tip. Or you could use a single large boulder as a base, cut flat and smooth on top. Either way, the base should be plenty wide enough to support the slab, even if someone were to sit on the edge of the table. It's a matter of proportion and weight to get enough support under the slab so that part extending beyond it won't have enough leverage to tip it. A thicker stone will stay in place better. A thickness of 6 inches is reasonable for a 5-foot-long table.

For extra stability, consider anchoring the tabletop with a headed steel rod down through a hole in the center of it. If you do this, the rod should be anchored solidly in the masonry below, at least 1 foot down, with perhaps a cross-bar welded into it so it won't pull out. You can countersink the hole in the tabletop so the head of the rod, or bolt, won't show when grouted in.

I'd leave the edges of the stone table natural, in whatever shape you like. A perfectly round or square or rect-angular table would sort of defeat its being made of a single stone, since it would look more like some imitation. A stone quarry can cut such a slab for you, and smooth and/or polish it, too. Granite is my favorite for such a use.

Barbecues

Outdoor cooking areas have become increasingly popular over the years, and the centerpiece of the outdoor kitchen is a good stone barbecue. Although many experienced masons like Toru Oba and Doug Bryant elevate the humble cooking station to a work of art, beginning masons can start by building a simple stone barbecue. No elaborate firebox is necessary; what you want is simply a place for the fire below the wire grill. More ambitious home masons may want to take on the challenge of adding a chimney to draw smoke away from the cooking area. Try personalizing your barbecue by selecting unusual stone, or even by mixing different types of stone. At the end of the day, you want your barbecue to be both functional and attractive. How you manage to destroy the steaks is up to you.

A Barbecue with Chimney

The same basic principles of building a stone fireplace and chimney apply to a stone barbecue too, although there are a few differences. A barbecue chimney is relatively short, for instance, so it won't draw quite as well. More height obviously helps; so will burning a newspaper back under the chimney to start getting the smoke pulled under there as it rises. You don't push smoke; you have to pull it with the vacuum left by that rising heated air/smoke.

Once you've built the base for your barbecue, you can begin the construction of the chimney, starting with the plywood form for the arch. Make it 24 inches wide and 8 inches high. Beginning 6 inches up the sides, scribe a curve that peaks at 8 to 10 inches. Cut out the form, then lay out a second form using the first for a pattern. Cut out the second form and nail the two together, separated by sections of 2×4 blocks. Lay the form on the ground and select and shape pairs of tapered stones to conform to the arch. Dry-fit the stones, allowing ½ inch of space for mortar between them and keeping the joints pointing toward a single focal point.

Once you've fitted the stones, set the form upright on the slab on wooden wedges for easy removal later, 30 inches back from the front of the side walls. Begin laying up the arch stones. Start with pairs of tapered stones at each end of the form, coating each side surface with ½ inch of mortar. Hold it back 1 inch from the front faces of the stones. Place these paired stones up each side of the arch form. Set the keystone last. Wait a

Doug Bryant combined granite, basalt, sandstone, and obsidian to build this barbecue, which has a Rumford-style firebox.

OPPOSITE: Toru Oba built this barbecue from field-gathered Pennsylvania sandstone.

day before removing the arch form, so the mortar will be solid enough not to compress.

Now blend the arch stones with more wall stones to a height above the top of the arch. The wedge-shaped arch stones will be irregular in relation to the wall's horizontal stones, so use odd-shaped stones to tie the arch and the rest of the stonework together, getting back to horizontal joints.

Begin stepping in the side walls (corbeling) 2 inches at a step. You may also step in the front chimney wall if you like. You'll need only 8 inches square or so inside the chimney to carry the smoke, so the degree to which you step in the chimney is up to you. Stand back and eye the stepped-in section for what looks good to you. If you take in the chimney too far, it'll look spindly; if you leave it too big, it'll be hard to heat up the volume of air inside to draw up the smoke.

Chimney height is optional. Usually 8 to 12 feet of overall height is proportionate. If you want a decorative bead, or rim, near the top, as in many older house chimneys, use stones 2 to 3 inches thick that will jut out 2 inches, within 6 inches of the top. Use bead stones deep enough to stay in place as you lay them. The weight of the stones above the beads will hold them, but you may have to set a temporary weight on the stones to keep them from tipping as you lay them, until the mortar hardens.

This artful structure, made from Toru's carved slabs of Culpeper granite and soapstone, supports a grill and countertop.

Stone Barbecue

A simple stone barbecue is a three-sided structure with a platform on which to build the fire and elevated sides for the wire grill. Orient it so that the front faces into the prevailing wind.

[1] Dig a footing ditch 12 in. wide in a C-shape, with each side of the C 42 in. long. The depth should be below the frost line.

Mix the footing concrete in a wheelbarrow, with enough water for a mix that will run when worked. Start with 2 shovels of Portland cement, 4 shovels of sand, and 6 shovels of gravel; mix additional batches until you have poured a footing at least 6 in. deep into the ditch. (A deeper footing will require more cement, sand, and gravel.) Keep it damp for at least two days, while it cures.

footing below frost line

[2] To mix mortar, begin with 9 shovels of sand, 2 of cement, and 1 of lime, plus water (see Mixing Mortar for Stonework, page 111). Begin laying stones, 36 in. to a side; use stones that are 6 in. wide, and center them on the footing. You can use rough stones below grade, or you can substitute concrete blocks. At ground level, build a three-sided wall, 6 in. thick and 30 in. high. Use a stiff mortar mix to set the stones.

[3] Make a rebar grid. Cut 10 lengths of rebar, 5 of them 26 in. long to overlap the side stone walls by 1 in., and 5 of them 24 in. long. Lay out 5 identical lengths of rebar 6 in. apart, then overlay with the other 5 lengths, securing the grid with wire or string. Lay the grid across the walls, with the longer rebar lengths across the side walls. Set the grid far enough back on the rear wall so that you have a couple of inches' clear-

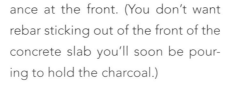

ance at the front. (You don't want rebar sticking out of the front of the concrete slab you'll soon be pouring to hold the charcoal.)

side wall

2×4 in front

rebar

plywood 2" below rebar

leg

[4] Cut a piece of plywood roughly 24 in. square and position it 2 in. under the rebar grid, wedging it into place. Use wooden wedges jammed between the edges of the plywood and the stone wall. Also support the plywood with four 2×4 legs, each set in about 4 in. from the edge of the plywood. Nail a fifth 2×4 to the front of the plywood to form a lip.

Add 6 in. of height to the three stone walls, either on top of the rebar ends or set back 1 in. so that the walls are 5 in. thick.

[5] Mix concrete, as you did for the footing, and pour it 3½–4 in. thick over the plywood form. Trowel it smooth, cover it with plastic sheeting, and keep it moist for four days.

[6] Remove the braces and the plywood and backfill around the stone walls with soil if you haven't already done so. The concrete slab is for the charcoal fire. Before using it, spread an inch of sand on the slab to protect it from extreme heat. Depending on the size of your grill, you can either set it on the raised stone sides of the barbecue or support it above the slab using extra wall stones or a few bricks.

There is nothing more natural than water moving over stone. The sound and sight of this phenomenon is a soothing reawakening of our earliest primal memories.

Water Features and Footbridges

And no matter how small or simple, the principle is the same: Get water to move or fall over stone — any stone — and you've created a calming, intriguing place for yourself and others to enjoy.

Water features come in roughly four categories: pools, fountains, streams, and waterfalls. About the only one that doesn't combine simply and naturally with the others is a fountain, because it so obviously is man-made and self-contained. (That doesn't make it a bad choice, though.) Any of these can be as varied as your imagination and skill will allow.

LEFT: When stone is carefully integrated into the landscape, man-made water features can look almost entirely natural.

Fountains and Pools

Although the term "fountain" may conjure grand images of Italian piazzas and water-spouting imps, small backyard fountains are actually fairly simple to build. You might be up for the task of pouring concrete, reinforced by rebar, and setting up an elaborate system for recirculating water. But really, a fountain can be as simple as a small pool hooked up to an inexpensive pump.

A simple reflecting pool at ground level, bordered by a stone rim, is where to start. Again, such a pool can be built as a concrete basin walled by a low stone rim, plastered inside. It can be any shape, but should be on a footing below the frost line, and be on a stable base, with reinforcing in the concrete. Alternatively, a small reflecting pool can easily be built with a flexible pond liner (see A Simple Garden Pool, at right). One word of warning: If you choose not to recirculate the water with a pump, the pool will likely get stagnant and provide an ideal place for mosquitoes to breed. To combat this, build the pool large enough to hold goldfish, which will eat the mosquito larvae, or use Bt (*Bacillus thuringiensis*) donuts, available at all retailers that carry water-gardening supplies.

This water feature in a Pennsylvania garden pairs natural unshaped stone with large pavers and a few artistic flourishes.

A Simple Garden Pool

A small pool can be a simple addition to a garden. Install a recirculating pump for aeration if you want minnows or other creatures to inhabit it. The pool is relatively maintenance-free; leaves can be raked out and the water siphoned out for cleaning, if needed.

[1] Dig the pool to a depth 3 in. deeper than the finished pool will be, making sure you're below the frost line. Make the diameter of the hole 5 ft. Let the bottom curve up to form the sides.

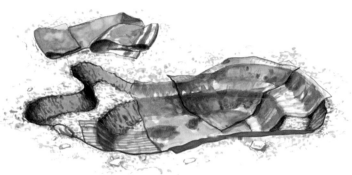

[2] Line the entire bowl with 3 in. of damp sand and a layer of geotextile underlayment.

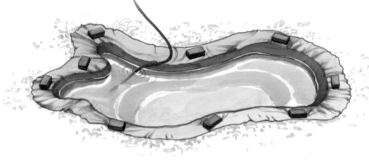

[3] Lay a flexible pond liner loosely into the hole, leaving an overlap along the lip of the pond. Place a few stones or bricks to hold the liner in place as you begin to fill the pond with water.

[4] After ensuring that the pond liner will hold the water, tightly lay shaped fieldstones around the edges of the pool. Backfill the spaces between the stones with soil.

Streams

To enjoy a more natural-looking source of moving water, consider building a stream. To keep the water from leaking away, you'll use an impervious liner, available at garden supply shops or building supply stores. Dig a meandering downhill-sloping ditch with a more-or-less V-shaped bottom. Begin at some logical starting point for the water, which could be a jumble of stones or a small pool at the base of some shrubbery.

Bend the watercourse around logically placed or natural features such as boulders, plants, or curves in a path. Widen it, narrow it — whatever suits your eye — but be sure it's not so wide that the liner can't cover the base of the stream and extend out a foot or more on both sides. As you dig, save any sod you remove for replanting later. Pile the dug-out soil off to the side, not next to the streambed; you want the stream banks to be even with the surrounding grade.

Liners aren't infinitely long, so you'll need to overlap the pieces (uphill over downhill, of course). Make long overlaps so water won't run back under them and escape. I like a 4-inch drop in the streambed at each overlap, so surges won't get uphill there. It's hard to bend the liner without wrinkling it, but that's not a problem. A black liner, with maybe some sand or pebbles at the wrinkles, won't be too noticeable.

If possible, lay out your watercourse in a dip or little swale so it'll look natural. You may have to create this by digging down in some areas and building up others, using the soil you've dug out elsewhere. When you line the watercourse, and anything else, make sure there are no sharp rocks under there; they could puncture the liner. It's a good idea to line the streambed with sand before you put in the liner.

Wherever your stream reaches its downhill end, you'll need a small pool, and a pump to take the water back up to the beginning. Bury a black plastic pipe with an inside diameter of at least ½ inch alongside the streambed. Attach the lower end of the pipe to a submersible garden pump that's designed for constant operation, and set this in the pool, which you will have lined. The upper end of the pipe doesn't need a nozzle, but you'll need to loop it in the ground so it faces in the right direction: downstream. Hide the end of it under a propped-up, mossy stone or other camouflage, but don't restrict the flow.

Now you'll need to weigh down and cover the edges of the liner at the pool and along the stream. This is the place to use the pieces of sod you removed when you dug the streambed. Laying a weathered stone on the lip of the liner here and there provides visual interest and extra stability. It also makes the stone look more like a part of the natural surroundings, especially if you use stone that's native to your region.

OPPOSITE: This constructed stream in a suburban neighborhood looks like a natural part of the landscape.

Recirculating the Water

Run electric wire underground to the pump, with a switch in your garage or garden shed. Bury this wire, and the water pipe, at least 1 foot deep so future gardeners won't cut them by accident. There's a special UF grade of wire for underground use. For a small pump less than 100 feet away, use #14 or #12 wire.

If you want more flow, the little pump won't handle it, and you'll need larger pipe and a bigger, separate motor/pump. Do screen the intake pipe in the pool for a separate pump, and set this pump, wherever it is, below the pool level to keep it primed. An air space will stop the flow.

A certain maintenance factor is present in any man-made water feature, and a watercourse has lots of chances to pick up debris. A submersible pump will have a built-in screen, but you should check it and/or the pickup screen often. A big pump will suck things like twigs and frogs up against the screen often. I've tried putting filters in the feed pipes of fountains and waterfalls to keep things clean, but they clog up quickly.

A fairly efficient filter is a natural one made of sand and fine gravel. It requires a fairly flat place in the watercourse, or more than one, where this material won't get washed off downstream. Build up some sort of barrier with small spaces in it to force the water to go through the fine gravel and sand to get downstream. If it's moving slowly here, the water will sink down and filter itself through this. The longer the stretch of sand/gravel you can build, the more it'll filter. But a heavy rain will cause this to wash down, eventually. Lining the barrier with a piece of filter fabric or a section of silt fence that lets the water go through but not the debris can sometimes be camouflaged enough to hold the material but not look ugly.

WILDLIFE LIKES WATER, TOO

BE AWARE THAT A WATER FEATURE is a magnet for birds and other wildlife. I view their visits as a compliment, a sign that I've created an ideal habitat for them. Some of the creatures, such as frogs, foxes, raccoons, and squirrels, are fun to watch; others, such as snakes, slugs, moles, gophers, groundhogs, and skunks, are less welcome. You have to take the bad with the good.

My sister-in-law told us of neighbors in Wilmington, Delaware, who had an ornamental pool, right in the middle of suburbia. They'd put rare goldfish in it, and enjoyed it as the focal point of their landscaping, but the fish kept disappearing. They suspected neighborhood cats. Then one day they saw the real predator at work, a great blue heron that flew in from woods who knows how many miles away. It had spotted that tiny pool as a lunch buffet.

Waterfalls

For even more interest, you could add a waterfall to link your streambed to the pool at the end. It aerates the water, sounds great, and is a delight to the eye. Just lower your pool or raise the end of your stream as little as 6 inches for the effect. (Don't raise the stream beyond level, though, or the water won't flow.)

The Pool

The pool part of this combination can be a circle, square, or any other shape, with the edges of its liner hidden under attractive stones. Unless it's at the very base of a slope, you'll need to dig back into the hill a bit to create a level space for it. In this case, you might want to combine the pool with a retaining wall, to hold the soil on the cut-out part of the slope.

The Water Source

Use a natural swale, or dig one, to direct water down the slope and over the wall into the pool. If your watercourse goes just a short distance — say 10 feet or less — you might choose to put down a deep gravel base and spread a couple of inches of concrete on it to form your waterway, reinforced with metal lath or wire. A simpler method would be to use a plastic liner, as detailed in Streams, page 189. It's cheaper overall, easier to install, and isn't subject to cracking like concrete.

If you don't want to include a stream as part of this project, the water can originate just above the waterfall, as long as the pipe is sealed around and/or discharges onto a plastic liner. I like to simulate a natural spring as the source, among mossy rocks, maybe partially screened by plantings. A spring is a source of wonder as well as of water: all that cold, clear, very necessary-for-life liquid bubbling up from the ground.

The Waterfall Point

Regardless of its source, the water should flow over a single stone to create the waterfall. It's logical just to let it fall over an edge, but the water often won't do that the way you want. It tends to cling, then run back under to slide down the back wall of the pool. You'll want the liner behind those stones, going up, back, and under the stream liner, so you won't lose any water. But you won't get much of a fall,

Creating more than just a waterfall, this mason has practically reconstructed an entire hillside in stone.

STONE STYLE: Water Features

There are so many unique ways to feature water in the landscape, beyond the typical naturalistic pond, stream, or waterfall. Thinking about the site itself and the materials available there is often a source of inspiration for masons and artists. Here are just a few ideas for your own backyard.

Todd Campbell creates sculptural stone fountains for indoors or out.

Using enormous boulders, these homeowners have brought a tropical fantasy to life with this poolside waterfall.

In Vermont, garden designer Gordon Hayward used the circular foundation of an abandoned grain silo for his garden pool and an old millstone for the center of his fountain.

either. Even tilting the stone doesn't help much with a low flow. A sharp-edged stone here will help, because there isn't a surface for the water to cling to. You may have to cut the facing edge to a bevel to achieve this.

You could use a perfectly level stone and let the water drip off its full length. That can look like what's called a natural dripping spring, but it's almost soundless. You can find or cut a channel in the stone, experimenting until you get the flow and sound you want.

Avoid a single surge that spouts and splashes too much water out of the pool below. You'll lose too much water that way, and it resembles a wastewater runoff. It's a good idea to set mossy stones in the pool for part of the water to fall onto. One of these, propped or sloped, can also conceal the submersible pump. These pumps are fairly quiet, so they're not too distracting, and they're easy to install.

The pipe from the pump to the top of the water flow must come up over the liner, and it's not hard to conceal it among and behind the stones that form the sides of the pool. Bury it up to the source above, deep enough to avoid future picks and shovels. If you've used a separate, larger pump, you'll bury this pipe from wherever the pump is to the source. And, of course, the pickup pipe, too. This pickup pipe, if the pump is separate, has to come up out of the ground, through the stones that form the pool rim but over the liner, and down to a screen in the pool. Again, well-placed stones can cover it.

Careful stone placement is required at the waterfall point to achieve the right flow.

Stone Bridges

Getting across streams and gorges and narrow bodies of water of all kinds has been a near necessity for most of human history. During all that time, no building material has exceeded stone in durability, and few have in strength. While today's steel spans can be made incredibly strong, they are subject to corrosion, metal fatigue, and, ultimately, failure. Stone bridges, though they may not last forever, have a long history. And they're still practical today, for many uses.

The only real reason most bridges aren't built of stone today is the cost. (We're not talking the Golden Gate or Verrazano here, but let's not forget the historic stone London Bridge.) As wages have increased, the cost of quarrying and building of stone has gone out of proportion. Relatively cheap steel will span longer distances with much less mass, and can be built quicker.

Two large stone slabs create a simple bridge in this Asian-inspired garden.

For foot traffic and light vehicle use, however, stone is still practical — unless, of course, you, the mason, must be paid for your work. In that case, only an insistence on stone, regardless of cost, could justify it. So if we're talking beauty, art, appropriateness, even authentic restoration instead of dollars, bring on the stone.

No stonework you do will be more subject to the hammering of the elements than a bridge. Just the wear of moving water will erode mortar, and eventually the stone itself (in a few thousand years). Other wearing conditions are waterborne sand and grit, and the impact of flood-propelled limbs, trees, or logs if the span is over a big stream. The traffic pounding across the bridge year after year, whatever that traffic might be, is yet another source of stress.

Basic Stone Footbridges

Three feet is wide enough for a footbridge. If it's to be a high bridge, more than a couple of feet, make it 5 feet wide and bring up side walls on it so nobody falls off. The length will determine the best design, as will your ambition and skill level. We can go from very simple here to very complex.

The simplest bridge would be one long thick slab of stone laid level across the wash. Practically speaking, we're talking about a rectangular stone at least 6 inches thick, preferably freshly quarried and with no weak-

the air. This dampness eventually gets into other parts of the house, where it rots wood or turns shoe leather and other surfaces moldy.

Avoid this by insulating between interior stone walls and the outside with a vapor barrier on the living-area side of the insulation. This lets the air-particle-trapping insulation be the same temperature as the outside air and keeps the stone from getting damp. If the stone veneer wall won't be in contact with an exterior wall, then you don't need to worry about the vapor barrier and insulation.

Don't get carried away with interior stone veneer, at least until you see how you like the effect. A single wall, or parts of a wall, can be just as dramatic without being overwhelming. At our house, for example, we have two sections of restored post and beam, with hand-hewn major posts every few feet. The walls are recessed between these, so that the posts and the mortised angle braces stand out. Some of these spaces are done in stone veneer, while others are plaster. Too much stone here would have darkened the house too much, so my wife, Linda, wisely limited me to the occasional section. One section forms one wall of an L-shaped stairwell. The light fixture placed high on the perpendicular wall washes light down the stone wall, defining the shadows of the rock. Another stone wall section frames the bay window seat, clearly defining that space separately from the rest of the room.

This log cabin fireplace mixes local granite and sandstone. Under my guidance, this was an apprentice's first such effort.

Fireplaces

Fireplace faces are the most common uses of stone inside houses, and they give you the opportunity for all kinds of creative effects. For example, my friend the geologist Nick Evans had us restore a log cabin on his property in the 1980s. He had collected geologic sample stones from his years in the field and wanted us to use them to face the upstairs fireplace in his house. Master mason Dan Smith was working with me then, and he created the resulting work, which uses all accent stones. To see it is like viewing a geological display in a museum. Fireplace faces are also ideal for showing off your arch-building skills, either above the fireplace opening or in a small built-in warming oven to one side.

As with veneer walls, large fireplace faces built of stone can significantly darken a room, so you need to consider that as you plan. Sometimes, you can compensate with large windows, or by keeping the surrounding walls a light color; other times, you may need supplemental lighting. For instance, the Great Falls, Virginia, home of fabric designer and expert quilter Jinny Beyer has a dining room that is a restored log tavern, with a 1930s stone fireplace that takes up the entire end of the long room. The fireplace itself was quite dark, and a terra-cotta tile floor and a low ceiling made it even darker.

During our restoration of this section, we added a window in the stair corner and painted the ceiling between the overhead beams off-white to lighten the room, and to make it appear taller. The fireplace stone, however, still made that end of the room disappear into darkness, so we hid miniature track lights behind the last overhead beam to wash the stones with light. The angle of the light accents the irregular surfaces of the stones, heightening the effect of the third dimension. Interior stonework loses a lot of its effect if you can't see it.

BEYOND THE ORDINARY

THERE ARE MANY VARIATIONS on the basic fireplace and chimney. Some chimneys, for instance, don't narrow above the smoke chamber. Some are entirely inside the house, to radiate heat where it's needed, while others are half in and half outside. Some stone faces go up to the ceiling, and then the chimney drops back outside. There are even see-through fireplaces, which are virtually worthless as heat sources, with no back to reflect heat out into the room.

At this writing, we're completing a corner fireplace on the main floor of a new house. The full weight of the three-story chimney and the fireplace above sits on a 5-foot, steel-reinforced hollow square base on the basement level. The recessed hollow has a stove flue at the back of it. The stove itself is recessed into this hollow space and heats the mass of stone. On the next level (the main floor), the fireplace was rotated a one-eighth turn to face the living room from the corner. Both flues go up alongside each other in the chimney: the 12-inch-square flue tile for the fireplace and the 8×12-inch stove flue from below. The two flues sit on and against the smoke chamber corner-first. The double flue goes up through the second floor and then through the roof at the side of the house. This three-story chimney is entirely within the house, so the heat that flows through it stays inside.

Combining the stove flue and fireplace, as well as pivoting the face of the firebox differently on each floor, challenged our crew. The owner is delighted and has declared the project a complete success in both beauty and function.

STONE STYLE: Fireplaces

Builders have long used stone for fireplaces because of its ability to retain heat. In addition to this purely functional aspect, stone sets the aesthetic mood for an interior living space. Each mason has his or her own style and stone preference, and this comes across in the widely varied works they create.

Alan Ash used a blend of seven types of stone from the Pacific Northwest to create this Rumford fireplace.

Todd Campbell built this unique fireplace with locally collected rock.

Toru Oba used reclaimed sandstone from an old strip mine in West Virginia to build this fireplace and chimney.

Suzanne and Ron Dirsmith designed this rugged, split-face granite fireplace for The Sanctuary, a wildlife refuge in Illinois.

Hearths

A raised hearth at a fireplace is a wonderful place to sit. Make it about 16 inches high and at least 20 inches deep. Overhang the stone top about 2 inches at the sides and front. I like to round sharp edges of such stones (and those of stone tables, too) with a swipe of the grinder blade.

We used a worn millstone as the fireplace hearth in a local log cabin we moved and restored. Millstones are often used when the house has some connection with a former mill. I once used one that was broken in the original shaping, in a fireplace face, up above the opening. These stones continue to fascinate us, being the stone parts of elaborate, mostly wooden machinery that functioned for thousands of years.

Typically, we use 2- to 4-inch-thick flagstones for hearths, whether raised or flush with the floor. We allow for the finished height when laying the stone beneath. Depending on the desired look, these can be squared or left in natural shapes with minimal mortar joints. Hearthstones should be smooth enough for easy cleaning. Pocked stone surfaces, or those with fossils in them, create added interest, but they gather dust. Lichens will not survive on hearthstones. If you've built the fresh-air intake into the hearth, you'll need to cut out for, or build around, this opening. If the intakes are in the fireplace side walls, the hearth can be continuous.

Flagstone Floors

Flagstone can be laid as flooring in houses, even over a wooden subfloor. That requires closer joist spacing, though, so the floor doesn't flex; otherwise, the joints or the stones can crack. It's best for a masonry floor — flagstone, marble, mosaic, or slate — to sit on something more solid than wood. Our own house has a cut soapstone floor in one section, created with rejects from an old quarry. We filled the area within the foundation with crushed stone, then a vapor barrier of 6-mil plastic sheeting to prevent ground moisture from wicking up into the room. Over the plastic, we spread 2 inches of sand, and bedded the random soapstone in that.

Some people insulate under indoor stone floors because you get essentially earth temperature down there. It is true that winter heat will bleed down through the masonry. In summer, the mass of the floor will keep it somewhat cool. But if you've underlaid the crushed-stone base with plastic, as we did, the air spaces in it will act as insulation.

Flagstones for indoor use are thinner than those we use outdoors, so we mud-set (bed in wet mortar) most of them to leave no hollows underneath, and we grout as we go. (When grouting any flagstone, by the way, don't recess the joints, as you would on a wall or other vertical work. That should

OPPOSITE: Flagstone is a good flooring option for entryways; it's durable and relatively easy to clean.

be obvious, but it isn't — until you stumble on it the first time.) For our soapstone floor, we grouted with our usual masonry mortar mix: one part lime, two parts Portland cement, and nine parts sand, plus enough water for a very stiff mix. This floor has stayed stable for more than 20 years.

We had planned a heated floor and installed a 400-foot coil of water pipe under it, but have never activated it, due to Virginia's temperate climate. Once before, we had an electric cable-heated flagstone floor and really liked it. We had built a cabin for ourselves in Missouri in the 1970s, and we used 2- to 3-inch-thick slabs of limestone for the floor. Underneath it, we'd laid electric heat cable on a bed of crusher run. It made the floor warm underfoot, so we went barefoot on it in winter, and our toddlers curled up on it with their blankies for naps. (These days, you can install similar radiant heating cable under your stone floor.) We grouted with masonry mortar, and used two coats of masonry sealer on the stones. Periodically, we'd wax this floor, as we do the soapstone floor in our present house.

Flagstone in a Sunroom

Flagstone is beautiful used in an indoor atrium or sunroom, where it can be laid on the ground or on a concrete slab. A pool or waterfall in such a location needs stone around it, and this can duplicate outside landscaping.

A few years back, we built an elaborate house on several acres near Charlottesville, Virginia. We designed the house around a giant oak tree and laid a flagstone patio near the tree, in a curve to enclose but not strangle its roots. We used porous mortar as grout over dry-laid crushed stone that would let the roots breathe. The subsequent buyers of the house wanted

IN THE EARLY DAYS

EARLY BUILDERS IN THIS COUNTRY didn't use flagstone floors much, because their soft lime-and-sand grouting mortar eroded easily. When we dismantled and moved the historic Sowell house for its reerection at the Michie Tavern complex near Thomas Jefferson's home, Monticello, in 1994, the basement kitchen flagstone floor was loose stones. These were relatively flat slabs of limestone, probably from the Shenandoah Valley, over the Blue Ridge Mountains. Those nearer the walls were still intact, with about 1-inch joints. The stones were bedded in dirt and no trace of grouting remained. We grouted that floor with our usual mix. Sometimes close-fitting flagstone floors were laid, with no grouting at all. Laid on dirt, however, these often settled unevenly. A tightly laid floor on deep crushed stone should not move.

to enclose the patio with screening, a high ceiling, and a copper roof, so we did that. Now this screened porch added a whole new dimension for living space, focused on that giant tree. But we didn't seal the flagstone inside the porch area as we would normally have done, again to help preserve the tree's roots.

Flagstone around a Woodstove

A common use of flagstone or slate is as a protective base for a woodstove over the main floor covering. In working on historic houses, we often see burned pits in wooden floors where coals have spilled from open stove doors. If you lay stone under a stove, beef up that section of the floor framing by installing extra joists, either as "sisters" alongside them or between each existing one.

When a woodstove is near a wall, you might also want to use stone to protect it. If it's thick, heavy stonework, you'll need to cut through the floor, down to a poured concrete footing or to the masonry walls of the basement, to carry the weight. But if you use thinner flagstones up on edge, resulting in only 200 pounds or so, you can get away with setting it in mortar right on the floor, with 6-mil plastic or metal flashing between the stone and the floor. This is the only place I'd use such stones. In either case, use masonry ties nailed or screwed into the studs of the wall to lock the stones to it. You won't have much thickness here, so you won't be able to rake the joints deeply. Try to keep them narrow.

Other Interior Accents

You can accent the interior of a house or other structure with stonework in any way your imagination inspires you. Just remember that the weight of stone construction must be supported on a footing of some kind, down in the ground. And it must be anchored tight to whatever wall it's against with masonry ties. Too many people try to glue flat stones onto walls with just mortar and expect them to stay in place. Trust me: It won't work.

Archways

You may have seen kitchens with wide archways in old brick. They can just as easily be done in stone. Since an accent of this weight requires a substantial footing, it's best to incorporate plans for a stone arch into your building plans at the start of the project.

WATCH YOUR BACK

FLAGSTONE LAYING is by its nature a labor-intensive job. You should by all means wear knee pads and get used to bending. Back injury or pain is an all-too-common complaint among both amateurs and professionals on floor jobs. I suggest some serious stretching exercises before tackling this work. And don't try to do too much at a time. You must learn this about stonework: It should never be hurried. If you lay as little as one stone a day, don't let that worry you. That's one stone more than you had the previous day.

Masons from the Bennett Brothers Stone Company left this unusual sandstone countertop rough-finished for a more rustic look. To protect the stone, it was sealed with a thinned-down polyurethane.

Tables

For a simple project, consider creating a stone coffee table from a single, relatively thin slab of any kind of stone that's smooth. This can be cut from a quarry and even polished. Or it can be one found alongside a creek, worn smooth by thousands of years of flowing water. Or it can be a freshly split or natural flagstone. Support this with a wrought-iron frame or set it on two standing stones, slightly angled toward each other so they won't tip sideways.

Stone countertops can be attractive if they're of polished stone that resists staining. Granite is a current favorite, available in varied colors: red, brown, blue, green, gray, and black. Soapstone was common for drugstore counter-tops and other such applications before modern materials. Marble is sometimes used, but the white or gray natural to this stone is not popular among color-conscious folks. A frequent complaint from hom-eowners regarding some stone countertops is that it's hard to tell whether they're clean. Apparently dried hot sauce can resemble patterns in the stone. Another concern among builders is the fragility of the stone coun-tertops in transit. With the sink cutout weakening it, the stone slab is easily broken.

Wine Cellar

As I understand it from oenophiles (wine lovers), a wine cellar is simply a space in the ground to keep wine at earth temperature. Theoretically, it could be just a hole in the ground, or a bunker of concrete or blocks or brick, or something like a root cellar. But the very term implies something more artistic, more refined. And of course, it should be built of stone. If it's destined for racks of expensive vintages, why skimp on the construction?

We built a wine cellar into the basement of a stone house under con-struction. We left a section of the 20×44-foot basement unfinished, with the natural hill slope soil intact. A footing separates the basement proper from this high crawl space. We dug the soil back to form a small room that will be walled and roofed with stone. In effect, it's a three-sided space created by retaining walls and roof to hold back the soil.

I suppose the wine cellar could be built outside, into a hill slope like the root cellar, but one expects the cache for prized wines to be accessible from inside the house, down winding stairs to cool depths. If you don't have a basement that's exposed to the earth, you can open a basement wall and dig back into the slope outside the house.

The wine cellar size is up to you. A 6×8-foot space will hold a lot of bottles, but even that, with a 7-foot-high ceiling at the peak of a vaulted arch, is more than 200 square feet of stone wall and will take awhile to build. If you have plans for spacious aisles of wine racks, count on a long construction time.

Construction. The cellar should be laid mortared, with footings for the walls. Since there'll be inward pressure from the soil, the walls should be 1 foot thick, and that means the footing should be at least 18 inches across. Down this deep, you'll be in firm subsoil, so settling won't be such a problem.

Early on in the construction, you should plan to bury a perforated drainpipe in a gravel subfloor, leading out and down, to carry any water away. If you put in a solid floor, include a drain, for obvious reasons. That will mean a long, deep ditch here, out to a downhill slope.

Once up to wall height, which should probably be around 7 feet, plan a semicircular arched ceiling. It should span the short dimension. This vaulted ceiling/roof will be a three-dimensional arch, rather like a stone bridge.

When the stonework is complete, consider plastering the entire outside of the walls to help keep moisture from seeping into the wine cellar. The same mortar mix can be used: the one-lime, two-Portland cement, nine-sand formula you use for the stone.

When backfilling around the cellar with soil, add only a foot or so at a time, tamping as you go. If you fill the entire space around the cellar at once, it'll settle a lot; then when you fill more, it'll settle more. Make sure to get at least 3 feet of soil on top of the wine cellar to keep it cool. When backfilling is complete, top it with a layer of topsoil about 6 inches thick, so you can grow grass or other plants over the area.

Finishing. Back inside the basement, you'll want an arched doorway with stone around it. Anchor your doorjamb with bolts into the stonework

A homeowner in Connecticut built this stone wine cellar himself, an ambitious project for a beginner.

as you build. A heavy, arched wooden door with forged strap hinges is what you'll want here, maybe studded with heavy forged nails. And you'll want insulation on the door, because this is where you'll have heat loss/gain. You can sandwich Styrofoam between panels, giving you a thick, dungeonlike door. Cover the foam at the edges of the door with thin wood nailed over it. Don't oil the hinges, so it'll creak delightfully when you open it. A heavy forged latch with maybe an antique lock will complete the look of treasure inside.

ABOVE: Roger Hopkins carved the sculpture he calls "44 Dots" from a single black granite boulder.

ABOVE RIGHT: An embedded natural gas line fuels the flame in this fire pit.

OPPOSITE: This massive stone archway had to be split into three pieces in order to be transported. It is 14 feet tall and 16 feet wide; the individual slabs are 2 feet thick.

"Stone is the royal building block," says stone sculptor Roger Hopkins. "It has nobility, strength, and the durability to last lifetimes."

Roger's love for stone has its roots in a landscape business. He has no formal art training, which he counts as an asset: "I have no preconceived notions, no rules to break, and so I'm free to do what I want," he says. On an early landscaping job, a diamond circular saw blade being used to cut a serpentine edge into a bluestone patio proved irresistible. Roger was compelled to experiment with it by slicing portions off a small boulder that he'd found at the site. To his delight, the result was a birdbath.

The satisfaction of creating that first birdbath has, in the decades since, taken him to four continents, exploring the pyramids in Egypt and hunting for scholar rocks in the Chinese hinterlands, for example, in pursuit of craggy muses and materials. "Traveling is good when you're younger," he says. "And when you get older, you commit your life to your work."

One of his trips to Egypt was for the PBS series *Nova,* for which he and a team of Egyptian stonemasons re-created a miniature pyramid using only ancient Eqyptian techniques, in just three weeks. "The ancient Egyptians were on the original learning curve of building with stone," Roger says. "I found plenty of mistakes, but I also saw where they had corrected them."

Roger's sculptures take their primary inspiration from the ancient techniques of stone setting, which he researched on expeditions to the standing stones of the British

Isles. From this primitive source he has evolved an aesthetic he calls "primitive modern," which enables people to experience the grandeur of rock in much the same way he does — as a source of power. His wish is for people to interact with his sculptures in an intimate way: to experience what he terms the "force that comes from feeling them, touching them . . . I want the stones to overpower you!" he says. "I want you to feel dwarfed!"

Although he doesn't think of any single project as his hallmark, the feeling of massiveness is present in everything he does, from an installation of standing basalt monoliths to an arched entryway of giant granite slabs. For one client, he even designed and carved a stone hot tub out of an enormous boulder (see page 134). He also feels that being willing to take on problematic assignments has helped him learn and grow as a stonemason. "Many of the projects I've been handed were ones that other contractors couldn't figure out and refused to bid on," he says. "As a result of not being able to say no, I ended up with a lot of challenges."

Roger chooses stone that will blend with the colors and textures of the locale it is destined for. Hard stones like basalt and gabbro are good for outdoors (unlike marble), so that is what he prefers to work with, and the bigger the better. Since his first foray with the birdbath, he's come to utilize a wide array of tools, but says that a three-pound hammer "solves all of life's problems." His main objective is not to overwork a stone, rush the process of creation, or diminish it in any way ("you can't take it back," he says), but instead to find the organic evolution from its natural form into its artistic one.

I have no preconceived notions, no rules to break.

For millennia, stone has held up buildings, aqueducts, roofs, and ceiling spans. The strength was from the stone itself — not timbers, steel, or concrete

Structural Stonework

simply covered with veneer for appearance. Stone was and is the only inorganic material available that doesn't rot, corrode, burn, fall apart, or break easily.

It's still a good material for structures built today. A wall of well-laid stone on a good footing is structurally sound, though it may confuse building inspectors, many of whom are used to seeing only stone veneer in their daily work. In fact, the widespread use of veneer on foundations has led to odd building codes in some areas — like the requirement that stone foundations be 16 inches thick (while concrete block foundations can get by with a mere 8 inches). Nevertheless, a well-built stone foundation can bear the weight of a structure and stand the test of time.

LEFT: Master mason Lew French created this stunning piece of architecture for a homeowner on Martha's Vineyard, Massachusetts.

Choosing Stone for Structural Work

When planning stone weight-bearing walls, it's a good idea to use dense, strong stone. Granite, basalt, dense sandstone, and quarried limestone are okay, while soft, crumbly sandstone, slate, or deeply weathered or porous stone of any kind can crush under the structure's weight. A good rule is to use stone that's harder than the mortar that's laid. I'm currently cleaning up cut blocks of a very soft West Virginia sandstone recycled from a large barn foundation. When I knock the old mortar loose from the stones, it takes part of the stone with it. These long blocks will hold up a low wall nicely but wouldn't be suitable for the concentrated weight of structural work, such as narrow bases for a series of arches holding up an entire building or the weight of the whole house on a stone foundation.

This brings up an important principle: Stone *must* be laid in such a way that the weight is distributed over as great an area as possible. I'm reminded of a sagging log cabin atop the Blue Ridge in Virginia, set on the odd-shaped granite of the area. The old lime mortar had eroded, and the masons had not laid the stone horizontally. The chimney had fallen completely, and the entire back cabin wall and one end were supported 7 feet in the air by a single large stone jutting up from the ruins of the old basement wall. Only a 5-inch-square stone surface supported all those tons of

MORTAR FOR STRUCTURAL WORK

YOU'LL FIND A LOT of variations and proportions of mortar ingredients among masons. For many centuries the material was simply lime and sand, where mortar was used at all. (As a side note, there are several prominent masons around the world today who are promoting a return to lime-and-sand mortar. Master stonemason Patrick McAfee, from Ireland, is among them.)

Things changed around 1900, when Portland cement found a use in stonework because it was stronger. Eventually, many masons just used Portland and sand, with no lime at all. That makes a hard, unyielding mortar that can crack when it contracts, often taking soft stone or brick with it. It also looks very gray and darker than mortar with white lime.

Today most non-stone masonry is done with a pre-mixed masonry cement, which is roughly half lime and half Portland cement. That's fine for concrete blocks and brick, both of which are porous and absorb the moisture from the mortar quickly. The high lime content attracts moisture from the air and keeps the mix damp while the chemical action that results in strength proceeds. If allowed to dry out, though, the strengthening chemical action stops. The result is weak or crumbly mortar that jeopardizes your work.

I like more strength than the masonry mix provides, but I like the slower setting the lime affords, too. So when I prepare mortar, I use one part mason's lime to two parts Portland cement to nine parts sand. The quantity of water required to mix it varies, since the sand is often wet from being outdoors in the rain. I add just enough water to get a fairly stiff consistency, drier than that required for brick or block but not so dry that it won't bond to the stones. It should stand up, not run, but it should also not be crumbly.

weight. Needless to say, I didn't spend a lot of time under there. As things turned out, I didn't restore the cabin, either.

In structural situations, never use thin stones up on edge to carry weight. Always remember that all mortar will erode in time. Go back to the principle that each stone should stay where it's placed, even under great weight, without mortar. Then use the mortar principally as a filler, to distribute the weight by filling any voids.

Where there is discernible grain in the stone, it is particularly important to set the stones so the grain is horizontal. As I've said before, a stone can erode or split with the grain when it's under stress or subject to weather. Many old stone chimneys and walls contain vertical-grain rocks that split off layer after layer until what's left crushes under the weight.

The pattern work on this round house in the Chachapoyan region of Peru is also found at the base of ancient ruins. The cantilevered stones above serve as a walkway.

ROCK STAR | Opus 40 SAUGERTIES, NY

Among the remains of an old bluestone quarry in what Manhattanites call "upstate" lies a six-and-half-acre masterpiece in dry-laid stone. It's called Opus 40, and it's the result of 37 years of work by one man, Harvey Fite.

Fite, a theater professor at nearby Bard College, bought the abandoned quarry in 1938 for a mere $250. After traveling to Honduras and helping to restore the Mayan ruins at Copán, Fite began to wonder if he could apply ancient Mayan building techniques to stonework using his own store of bluestone.

What began as an intended display ground for outdoor sculptures eventually became a sculpture itself — an environmental installation of massive proportions. Fite worked on the project during his off hours, laying stone with only the simplest of tools: a chisel, a stone hammer, and a hand-powered winch. As the project grew and began to attract media attention, reporters and admirers pressed Fite to name his masterpiece. He finally relented, calling it Opus 40 because he thought it would end up taking 40 years to build (he wasn't far off).

Fite died in an accident at the quarry in 1976, at the age of 72, before completing work on the project. Today, Opus 40 is operated by Fite's stepson, Tad Richards, as a nonprofit organization and is open to the public.

For contact information for Opus 40, please turn to page 265.

Foundations

For building foundations, it's often necessary, and always advisable, to set anchor bolts into the top stone layer for bolting the sills into place. Building codes require that the sills be of pressure-treated wood or that a termite shield of metal flashing be used between wood and masonry. Not only do these practices discourage bugs from getting into the wood, but they also keep moisture from wicking up through the masonry from the ground and causing decay.

It sounds backward, but I have built the foundation of a log cabin or timber-frame structure (the only kinds I build) by building just the stone corners to hold the sills, and then building the rest of the foundation later after the house is up. To get this top course of stone level and even, it's a good idea to secure the sill at the right height and build the stone up to it. I nail the metal flashing to the underside of the sill, drill holes, and hang the anchor bolts from the suspended sill, then space the stones to fit around the bolts and use mortar to get everything even.

I prefer copper for flashing because it takes on a nice patina over time. Aluminum or galvanized metal works too, but it stays shiny. You can cut your own flashing from a roll or sheet of metal or buy 8-inch-wide, precut material for that purpose. The longer the piece of flashing, the better, but you can use overlapped shorter pieces with careful installation.

This dry-laid granite foundation supports a restored log tavern in Virginia. The oak sill log spans the crawl space opening, making a lintel unnecessary.

Wall Openings

Obviously, a solid stone wall of the necessary thickness is the best support for any structure above it. We often want doorways, windows, arched openings, or other holes in that wall, however; that means shifting the load to either side to create the opening. The weight above the opening can be supported by a lintel, arch, straight keystone span, or inverted V.

Lintels

A lintel is the simplest span over an opening in a wall. It's a horizontal member (beam of wood, steel, precast concrete, stone, or log) supported by the sides of the opening, carrying the weight above it.

Ancient builders also struggled with the problem of how to support wall openings. You see simple vertical wall ends with massive lintel stones across, or stones leaning into each other all the way to an apex above, or the modified version of this — the inwardly sloped sides of the opening topped with a shortened lintel. The Lion Gate at Mycenae on the Greek island of Argos is an example of this, as are the doorways and windows of some Peruvian buildings. The shorter lintel could and did carry more weight and required a shorter stone. Obviously, a long lintel stone is more apt to crack under weight.

Arches

The Romans invented arches, which, as in any other span, redirect the weight to either side, but do it in a less direct, curved path. Each wedge-shaped stone in an arch pushes out the weight to one side or another, then downward as the curved side of the arch comes down to the wall below. The outward thrust is less with a tall arch, more with a flatter one.

It would seem necessary for this opening to be surrounded by solid stonework so that these thrusting forces could be contained, but it isn't; they're redirected downward. The arch can be freestanding if it is a semicircle or steeper. If flatter, the outward push is greater, since the center of the arch exerts more pressure. It's a form of leverage so, yes, it needs some lateral bracing. The same principle applies to a ridged roof. The flatter the pitch, the greater the outward thrust from the roof weight. A steep roof pushes downward harder and outward less.

A heavy, flat lintel stone spans the opening in this oldest of arch treatments.

In a triangular arch opening, two side stones are sloped together; weight still bears against and onto each side stone.

The semicircular arch transfers all the weight from above to each side and is perhaps the strongest span.

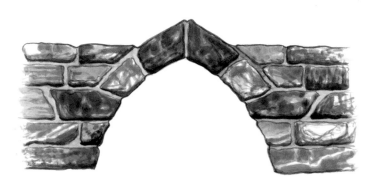

A Gothic arch is mostly ornamental, but is also strong, carrying weight on each side.

Todd Campbell used a triangular arch for the decorative end of this culvert.

Flat Keystone Spans

A flatter arch approaches another type of opening, the flat keystone span. This is just what the name implies: a lintel-like horizontal span of stones that is self-supporting, even though it's made up of pieces. Like an arch, it requires a form or temporary brace until the keystone is set. Here, outward thrust is at its greatest, and only the shapes of the stones carry the leveraged thrust to the sides. Ideally, all of the stones should be wider at the top than at the bottom, although all but the keystone and the two end stones can be rectangles (actually, parallelograms). If the end stones are braced with other stonework and the keystone is set, the entire span holds in place. For it to fall, it must compress the masonry to each side, and if properly laid, that won't happen.

Nowadays, arches aren't used as often as they once were over windows and doors, but when they do appear, flat or flatter arch spans are usually the style, especially in brickwork. Whether in brick or stone, this span is often reinforced with an angle-iron brace under it.

In some instances, masons take the weight off a flat span by building filled-in arches above it. That way, only the few stones between the flat span and the supporting arch bear on the span. I saw these often in Scotland.

A rim or partial diameter arch spans an opening with less height than a semicircular one. It is favored for window, door, and fireplace openings.

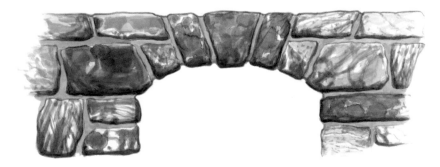

Structural Arches

An arch in stone is a thing of beauty. Along with its grace, there is the sometimes subconscious appreciation by the observer of the craftsmanship that created it. Even in a place where other superb stonework abounds, an arch becomes the focal point. An arch takes you through the wall, either physically or visually. What is beyond that massive wall is accessible through that opening, and it calls to you. Light, and other views, comes through an arch. The space on one side of the wall is doubled with that one opening. What was contained is now allowed freedom, and not just through a simple gap in the wall — rather, through a symmetrical, balanced bit of architectural achievement, still with a hint of structural mystery.

Throughout history, since their invention by Roman builders, arches have conveyed a sense of achievement and something of passage. Triumphal arches commemorated military victories and conquests and only

MORE ABOUT ARCHES AND SPANS

OVER THE CENTURIES, arches and spans have played a major role in stonework. Sometimes, wall builders wanted to allow as much air flow as possible, or to reduce the mass of what would otherwise be a solid wall. The aqueducts engineered by the Romans are one example: the object was to hold up a horizontal watercourse using as little stone as possible. The result was high, open semicircles of stone, culminating in a continuous trough for the water. Like bridges, these arches were necessary only to span low places, so the entire aqueduct didn't require stone support. Where trenches could be dug, they were. And where the contour of a hill could be followed, it was. The object was to keep the water flowing and get it to the cities, where it supplied households, fountains, and gardens.

Where a roof or ceiling was to be supported, the early builders started out with what amounted to a three-dimensional span. That's how Greek temples and Inca public buildings were built, and even in prehistoric structures we see the remains, such as Stonehenge, which probably was a building originally. Stone columns or walls supported lintels for a continuous periphery, which in turn supported roof or ceiling beams of wood.

Sometimes these beams joined above interior columns or walls to allow larger structures while keeping these spans short. (That's basically how we build today, by the way, whether with masonry or wood or steel; we put up a supporting exterior, then construct floors, ceilings, and roofs off that exterior structure, spanning horizontally between walls to create and enclose interior space. We seldom use stone as the support walls now, but the principle is the same.)

The Romans came up with innovation here too, applying the two-dimensional arch to the business of interior space. The resultant three-dimensional arch created a vaulted ceiling, much used for covered walkways. Even rooms could be built this way, with doorways in the arched openings or some other subwall material filling them. A three-dimensional archway creates an angled line from each of its four bases up and over and down to the one diagonally opposite. These lines describe other, wider arches. Such vaulted arches have been much favored as gazebos in the classic tradition. I recall a masterful example in York, England, which actually had been a stable under a church originally.

symbolically led anywhere. Open courtyards were often bounded by series of arches that did not keep people in or out but still provided a sense of entering and leaving the space.

Covered, arched passageways can be especially beautiful. Besides letting in light while sheltering those who walk underneath, arched stone passageways give an entirely different feel from similar structures with columns or posts. The very necessity of structural strength creates the mass stone needs to be visually correct.

Of course, you don't need to create massive structures to include arches in your stone projects. A feature as small as a 12-inch arched warming oven in a stone fireplace face becomes a focal point of the stonework. A miniature arched window in a crowded kitchen wall or an arched niche where something special can be displayed has a similar effect.

An arch is a challenge to build, but aside from its technical aspects, this structure requires some sense of design. There are several kinds of arches, including semicircles, elliptical, catenary, and partial-circumference (rim) types. Deciding on the best type of arch for a particular site and effect requires training, experience, and a natural, artistic eye.

I have built semicircle fireplace arches to mirror arched windows because owners wanted them, but I have seldom felt this design was as pleasing as a flatter rim arch. On the other hand, I find an ellipse over a wide doorway in a house is often more attractive than a rim. A semicircle, too, is often the best arch for windows and doors in stonework house walls. Again, a lot of this is subjective.

When early builders in the eastern United States constructed an arched fireplace, their custom was to use 13 stones — six on either side of a prominent keystone — to represent Jesus and the twelve disciples. Supposedly, Peter and John were the anchor stones. Today, most fireplace arches consist of fewer, wider stones.

This solid stone arch is one of several openings forming a portico along a recessed porch on a house under construction.

One of the arches at the 12th-century Dysert O'Dea Church in County Clare, Ireland, is made up of the carved faces of humans, dogs, and birds.

This natural-appearing opening shows the principle of the cantile-vered collapse that occurs in caves. Dan Snow duplicated it nicely.

Cutting an Arch

Building an arch requires stones in shapes that you will very rarely find in nature. Each stone should be tapered, with its sides all pointing to one spot, which means you'll have some cutting to do (see page 50). For a semicircular arch, that spot will be the center of the circle. For a partial arc such as in a fireplace face, the point will be somewhere in the space, but still the center of the circle this rim represents. In an elliptical arch, in which the ends curve more than the center, the target point of the stone sides is higher, nearer the stones themselves.

Regardless of the kind of arch you plan to build, you'll need a form to set the stones. I make my forms out of plywood, using two pieces with their tops cut to match my arch. I separate the two pieces with 2×4 or 2×6 blocks to give the form some depth, set it on wooden legs, and then wedge it in place so I can remove it later, when the arch has been set up and mortared.

The arch is built on a removable form with shaped stones set so that they wedge into place, transferring weight from above to each site.

You can mark lines on your form and then cut the stones to fit the lines, or you can do as I do, matching pairs of stones from each end. I come up the sides with these pairs, and then tailor the keystone to fit the last space left. Either way, the sides of each stone still must be shaped to lead to that common point.

If your arch is deep, you may have to use two stones from front to back. If you do, have every other stone be long enough to span the full depth of the arch, just as you'd use tie-stones in a wall. The recessed porch we built on a stone house in Keswick, Virginia, had five 42-inch-wide arches that were 9 feet tall and 14 inches thick. Each arch required 17 stones, all shaped and interlocked. To keep it strong, every other arch stone was full-depth, alternating with the doubled ones. We laid them out on the ground, cutting each to fit around the arch form. This form was later set up between the columns to support the precut stones, laid up in pairs, and mortared in place until the keystone was set. The form could theoretically come out immediately, because the mortared arch was supported by the columns and gravity pressed the stones against each other.

Keystones in arches or in flat keystone spans inevitably draw the eye, and should be well done. Sometimes masons allow the keystone to "stand proud," or extend an inch or so out from the front arch plane. Often the keystone is taller than those around it. It should never be smaller, or it loses a lot visually. Here's where careful shaping will give you what you want. You can, of course, keep hunting until you find just the right arch stones you won't have to cut, but you'll be far older by the time you're done, and you'll need to choose from many, many stones. Such uncut stones leave you with a rustic, more natural look, however, which can't be all bad.

ABOVE LEFT: Fred is seated at the base of a set of steps at the entrance to the Jomeo-kee Trail in Pilot Mountain State Park, near Winston-Salem, North Carolina.

ABOVE RIGHT: The Jomeokee Trail is lined with large stones called gargoyles, which serve to keep visitors on the trail

OPPOSITE: Mortared stone columns support handrails at Pilot Mountain State Park.

"Our track dump truck — we call her Ursula — carries five thousand pounds," boasts Frederica ("Fred") Lashley of her IHI IC-30 (which, like all of her fueled equipment, runs on biodiesel). Ursula hauls the surfacing for backcountry trails, which are among the many things Fred and her company, The Unturned Stone, build.

This self-described "educated itinerant" set her first stone in 1988 while volunteering with a crew on the Appalachian Trail. "Somewhere along the line I realized I wasn't well suited to work for someone," Fred says. Knowing firsthand that masons are a "bunch of independent-minded people," as she puts it, Fred made her business goal to develop a long-term supportive culture of kindred craftsmen — who have chosen masonry "for its limitless potential" — within which her two teams of employees (residential and trail) can be inspired to work.

Fred is currently one of three female members among 100-plus in the Professional Trailbuilders Association. "I'm a good mason," she says, "but I'm really, *really* good at trails." Her present project, the Ledge Spring Trail in Pilot Mountain State Park, has been covered in "social paths" — that is, unbuilt trails naturally formed by hikers over time. The Unturned Stone is now converting those two miles of trail. The aim of a project like this is to consolidate the existing pattern of trails into one well-traveled path. Focusing foot traffic onto one trail reduces erosion and protects the surrounding

environment. Considerations include step height, tripping hazards, and the grade of the climb, not to mention how to transport the timberwork and boulders up the mountain without destroying the underbrush.

Fred gives credit where credit is due: she applies boulder-transportation techniques developed by Maine-based Trail Services proprietor Lester Kenway. Kenway adapted a system for pulling and lifting heavy loads using hand-powered winches. Originally designed for lowering and raising window washers on skyscrapers, Griphoist winches are small, powerful, and easily hiked deep into the woods. All of her materials have to be "backpack-able," Fred says, including 100-foot-long, 70-pound wire and rigging equipment.

If you do the job right, it blends in.

"If you do the job right, it blends in," she says. "People don't realize that half the rocks they're looking at were hauled by hand on two high-lines," or that it possibly took two or three days to get ten stones in place, especially if Fred and her crews are not allowed to use stone found outside the trail corridor. (The fun days are when they get to import the stones by helicopter.)

As her company manifesto proclaims: The Unturned Stone is not a "lick 'em and stick 'em" stone company. Fred's hope is that their work will set a high industry standard that will be appreciated by their clients. "A well-informed client is a good client," she says. "We want to take the time to do it right, because we want to be able to be proud of every piece of work."

Domes, essentially a series of intersecting arches that support weight from above, are seen in sophisticated Roman architecture and humble root cellars in Kentucky.

Domes

The use of the arch progressed naturally to the construction of the dome, a pure application taken to its extreme. If an arched opening could still support weight from above, and if intersecting (vaulted) arches could give a support with depth, why couldn't one keep on building the arch from all sides and have a dome?

Nobody told the Romans they couldn't do this, so they did it. They discovered that a thicker base for the dome, where it starts its upward curve, had to be built to help hold things stable, so they did that too. The results were ultimately the domes and even the minarets with their onion tops in the Middle East and Russia.

I've seen the dome in perhaps its most rustic form. Root cellars built by pioneers in Virginia, Kentucky, and Tennessee were sometimes built of drystone, roughly shaped and laid flat. The builders would excavate a hillside, and then build the dome with circular courses of stone. Each course came up and in to form the three-dimensional curve of the dome, which didn't need a form if laid carefully. The trick was to corbel, or overhang, each course just a little, so it didn't tip. Soil was built up around these stones to help hold them in place. Then, with the curve of the decreasing hole left as the builders went up, there was bracing against each stone from the side. This hole got smaller, until at last one capstone covered it.

These enterprising masons then shoveled dirt back onto the top of the dome to get a mass of earth. With a thick covering of soil, the structure maintained earth temperature (about 56°F) — ideal for storing potatoes, onions, carrots, and other things the pioneers needed to keep cool. Because it's belowground, the structure also keeps things from freezing.

Columns

Once you've gained some confidence by building walls, you might want to try your hand at building stone columns to support a porch floor or roof. This is a seemingly simple project, but it's demanding in its own way. Almost every other stone is a corner, meaning it has not one face, but two, in addition to the ideal flat top and bottom. And the corners have to be square. That means a lot of shaping.

I recently donated the work and materials for a pair of fieldstone columns at a new church, to support the peaked pediment roof entryway. The columns were 9 feet tall and 2 feet square. To go ahead with getting the roof on, the builders had set steel pipe posts on wide footings below the frost line, leaving me the bases for my stonework.

I was using the leftovers from several jobs, the small stones that didn't fit well anywhere. But I didn't want a rejected-stone look here, so I cut a lot. I was able to get volunteer help for part of the job from my friend Alex Rucker; my son, Charlie; and a couple of others. Each of us worked on a section of one column and then switched, to blend the work better.

Typically, on such narrow expanses, a corner stone would reach either all the way across a face to the next corner stone or (far more commonly) there would be one stone between. Since all four faces were visible, the challenge here became avoiding the same look repeatedly. We were also restricted from using deep stones by that steel pipe up the center.

We concentrated on varying the heights of each course and avoiding vertical running joints. Now and then, we could fit in a bigger accent stone, but most were from 2 inches to about 8 inches high. The temptation to stand up a lot of stones on edge was strong here, but we did that only for an accent stone, and only if it was thick enough, and only where there was no discernible vertical grain in the stone — in other words, not often. As we built up, we filled the core around the pipe with crushed gravel, where there was room. This center was sheltered under the roof and a mortar cap, so no water could get inside.

Every foot of vertical progress on such a column means 8 square surface feet of stonework. It requires really good stone in order to build four tight corners for each layer. Any deviation from the vertical will be noticed, and you can't have any bulges, curves, or recesses. As a beginner, you'll be

Because columns use so many cornerstones, it's important to select stones with at least two good faces.

pushed to do 8 square surface feet per day. I aimed for only about twice that and found it difficult. Still, the end result of a straight, attractive column is worth the effort you invest.

My masonry crew and I are also building a set of five 9-foot stone arches for a loggia, or recessed porch. These arches not only are part of the design but also support a 4-foot wall, which in turn supports about 20 feet of the roof rafter top plate. We began building the 9-foot piers with solid stone, but to get the roof on the house sooner, we set steel pipes to carry the weight, and built the last two arch piers around the pipes. Even though we had to use smaller stone around the pipe supports, choosing and placing them carefully, with an occasional (necessarily shallow) full-length stone, this allowed us to produce work that was almost the same as the solid-stone parts.

Chimneys

One of our most frequent stone construction projects is the building of fireplaces and chimneys. While few people rely on fireplaces for heating today, it seems everyone wants one. Nothing warms the atmosphere like the dancing flames of a fire. And certainly a stone fireplace and chimney add greatly to the value of even a modest house.

The Footing and Base

Building a chimney begins with the footing. A chimney is essentially a column of stone with a concentrated load of 20 to 40 tons resting on an area as small as 3 by 5 feet for a 36-inch fireplace. Unlike a column, though, a chimney is hollow, so its weight is greater around the periphery. A chimney needs a stronger, thicker footing than that for a wall, which spreads out the weight more. The footing should be steel-reinforced concrete and 1 foot thick, extending at least a foot out from the chimney itself in all directions. The idea is to spread the weight across the pad and to keep the chimney column from settling.

This footing must be below the frost line, which varies a lot across the country. The purpose is to get below the level where the earth moves when the soil freezes and thaws. In central Virginia, that level is

The base for this raised-hearth fireplace shows filled concrete block underlayment, over which firebrick for the firebox will be laid. This complicated chimney has two flues: one for the basement wood-stove flue (shown) and one for the upstairs fireplace being built. A pipe for the fresh-air duct brings outside air into the fireplace for better combustion.

The Chimney

Outside, traditional chimneys taper from the 5-foot width we're talking about here to about 3 feet, either in steps or at a slope, often matching the house roof pitch at the gable end above. As you go up the house wall, building codes require you to keep the masonry 2 inches from the framing. That'll mean later scribing a piece of siding or wood trim to the stonework, and some caulking to keep out rainwater. Keeping out rainwater is tricky and especially necessary at the taper of the chimney. Here you must add flashing as you build up the stone. I recommend flashing with copper, which takes on an attractive patina over time. You will also need flashing at the roof, usually with step-flashing on the slope and straight flashing at the roof overhang.

Building codes require that the height of the chimney be 2 feet above a metal roof peak, or 4 feet above wooden shakes if the chimney rises at the peak. If your chimney is at the side of the roof or anywhere off-center of the roof peak, check your local building codes. The correct height is necessary both for fire safety and for protecting the chimney's ability to draw the smoke. If the top of the chimney is too short, the shape of the roof can cause a wind effect, which will interfere with the chimney's drawing.

Remember: The taller the chimney, the better it draws, because there's a taller column of heated air and smoke rising. That's why smokestacks were and are built so tall. A very short chimney just won't carry up a large volume of heat, and stray winds can blow down it, even if the smoke shelf is right. Avoid angling chimneys or installing horizontal flues.

Stone Houses and Outbuildings

Stone houses have been built since our earliest ancestors stacked rocks to form walls and roofed them with poles and animal hides, thatch, or sod. The walls did not rot or catch fire, and the spaces between the stones could be plastered with mud or clay to keep out the elements. As the skill of these early masons grew, they shaped the stones with harder hammerstones, so that they fit tight. These sheltering walls could be reroofed as needed and stood for thousands of years, or until some conquering tribe destroyed them.

Variations on this basic structure served as the most permanent of dwellings until well into the 20th century. This was when people got serious about heating whole houses and had to worry about issues like heat loss and gain. As our standard of living climbed, we wanted to be able to be inside without heavy clothing. And we didn't want all that heat going outside through the walls in winter or coming inside in summer.

So we learned about insulation, which architects and builders such as Thomas Jefferson had experimented with 150 years earlier. They used brick fill, or even sand and plain dirt fill, in walls and over ceilings to slow the flow of heat. Straw would have been better, but being so flammable, nobody wanted to use it. But yes, those thatched roofs did hold heat; maybe there was something to this insulation business.

OPPOSITE: Legacy Stoneworks built this granite house in New Jersey. In houses like these, the interior chimney is usually built along with the house stone wall.

Before refrigeration, perishables were often kept cool in stone spring houses like this one.

Stone and brick houses were tight and kept out drafts, but they tended to be damp. And the heat did go through those walls, even if it didn't go quickly. The dampness came from the moisture that condensed from the air on cold masses when heat, as from the sun, hit them, or from any sharp temperature change. Thus, even when plastered nicely on the inside walls, these houses weren't all that comfortable.

The Stone Veneer House

Nowadays, most stone or brick houses are really just covered in masonry, with the structure of wood, steel, or concrete underneath. That allows both insulation and a vapor barrier in the walls, and the heating and air conditioning bills go down. There's nothing wrong with a stone veneer house, except that it's about the most expensive one you can build. You're actually building a complete house, minus the outside skin, basically as you would one of clapboarding, board-and-batten, stucco, hardboard, vinyl, or aluminum siding. Then you're covering it with stone, which costs more than any of these other coverings. In the long run, though, stone increases the value of the house far beyond what it costs for the stonework.

A True Stone House

Let's not forget about those structural masonry houses that served so long and, comparatively, so well. Could you build one today? Yes, you could.

First of all, let's address the problem of insulation. The highest heat-loss area in any home — stone or not — is the roof or attic, because heat rises. The next problem areas are windows and doors, which are also the same in any house. You cut heat loss through any roof with insulation. It's more difficult to control heat loss through wall openings, but using storm doors and double-glass windows will help in any type of dwelling.

So the big issue with solid-stone construction is the walls, which must be insulated and sealed to keep out moisture. Can we keep the heat in and the dampness out? And still spend less money? Yes and yes.

Think about the way we finish basements of concrete or block. We use masonry nails to attach furring strips, usually an inch or two between them, to the walls. Then we insulate with foam board maybe 2 inches thick, and use plastic sheeting for a vapor

This stone house, constructed of round boulders that do not sit easily upon each other, must have been a challenge to build. The success of the house is due entirely to the talent and artistry of the stonemason.

barrier, before using whatever sort of interior wall covering we've chosen. All of these materials, plus the mass of the basement wall itself, hold heat well. We can use the same materials to insulate interior aboveground stone walls. Minimal house wall insulation, of no more than 3 or 4 inches, plus a thick, tight stone wall, will cut a lot of heat loss.

You may find yourself at odds with your local inspections office regarding building codes if you build a solid stone–walled house. Almost no one does this anymore, so the bureaucrats there won't know what table or chart or label to apply to you. If this is to be a dwelling, they may require you to overbuild a lot (using 16-inch stone walls, for instance, where ordinarily 8-inch block is okay), and to overinsulate, too. Still, the result can be worth the hassle.

Sheds

Workshops and storage buildings, too, rise to a higher level of attractiveness, value, and permanence when built of stone. A grouping of well-built stone outbuildings appeals to our love of good construction, beauty, and often history.

The round stone barn at Hancock Shaker Village in Pittsfield, Massachusetts, was designed to facilitate feeding and milking cows.

Essentially, a stone shed is just four walls and a roof, so it can be a good structure to start with if you want to attempt structural stonework. You may want to incorporate a window in a stone wall, although it's easier to do that in a wooden gable end. Of course, you'll need a door, and this opening has to be built in as you erect the walls.

Barns and other outbuildings are other good uses of structural stone. The main objective is shelter from wind and rain, and no material is as tight or long-lasting as stone. I'm reminded of the superb round dairy barn in Hancock, Massachusetts, built by the Shakers in the early 1800s. Not only is the craftsmanship excellent, but the design is efficient and beautiful as well.

Gazebos

No matter how inviting a landscaped garden is, no matter how many enticing paths, water features, focal points, and plantings it has, it's still outdoors, a place to enjoy on dry days only, and on days when it's not too cold or windy. A gazebo is an outdoor structure, open enough to let you see and enjoy the beauty around you, but roofed against drizzle, rain, and even snow. (Yes, you can enjoy a well-landscaped garden in the winter, if you're sheltered from the worst of the weather.) While a gazebo won't keep you totally out of the wind, it will make it possible for you to be out among your creations more of the time. Besides, it'll look good.

Beehives

A beehive in stone is a reproduction of an ancient storage place that was shaped like a beehive. It's open inside, built of drystack stone laid so it sheds water. Although most, if not all, of these being built by masons today are purely ornamental, you could certainly build your own to be waterproof and use it to keep things in.

The beehive is circular, with flat-laid stones that have just a slight slope outward to drain rainwater away. (Obviously, if this slope were significant, the structure would pull itself apart in time.) Each stone is held in place by those above it, even though these are corbeled in at the upper courses or overhung inside. The circular shape braces these stones, as a three-dimensional arch.

With such a legacy of masonry, with so many millions of stone structures in the world, it is essential that we learn to preserve them and perpetuate them.

Restoration Stonework

Whether you're restoring crumbling porch post supports or a sagging foundation on a fixer-upper, the process is the same as it was in centuries past. You need to brace whatever structure the stone is holding up, then remove and re-lay the stone. In some cases, it may be enough to simply repoint the joints with mortar. For drystone wall restorations, removing roots and vines to get to the problem is often the first step.

OPPOSITE: The mortar on St. John's Episcopal Church in Williamstown, Massachusetts, has been repaired many times over its 112-year life.

The sloppy repair work (at left) on an interior stone terrace wall in the Sacsayuaman fortress, Peru, doesn't come close to replicating the original Inca work (at right).

A few years ago, I watched modern-day stoneworkers in Agua Caliente, in Peru, shaping the white granite from the Urubamba River cliffs. They were part of the workforce employed in the rapidly growing tourist facilities for Machu Picchu. Rock dust hung in the air as men labored to produce thin rectangles of stone that would be stood up on their ends and mortared onto the faces of walls in monotonous rows.

The men worked with crude chisels made of rebar, which blunted often. There was a rudimentary forge on the site, and one man heated, hammered, and quenched these barely usable chisels to harden them as the others brought them to him. Rebar won't get very hard, I can tell you as a blacksmith. They used a variety of hammers that looked like a flea-market collection of mismatched castoffs.

One man's hammer intrigued me; it was of a shape I'd never seen in a life of make-do tools, coming as I do from one of the most rural parts of our country. I moved closer to see, just one of a throng of tourists moving along the colorful stalls of the vendors who lined the way. The man's hammer was actually a battered automobile screw jack. He was beating on the mushroomed head of his chisel with whatever part of the base of the jack he could, holding it by the top. His hands were masses of calluses, his bare arms covered in white dust. His concentration was total despite the crowded walkway of camera-toting gawkers just feet away.

I had never seen such a primitive work site. I sensed that this man, and all the others, probably knew that if production lagged, there were hundreds of others at the gate ready to take his place. My overriding thought was, *Can't somebody at least give this man a hammer?*

Maybe it had always been this way. Maybe 500 years ago the scene would have been much the same — with one major difference, however (besides that smashed jack). These men weren't shaping the amazing interlocking blocks of stone that formed the ruins crowning the peaks and ridges high above us. Each anonymous shape here would go into a veneer wall with thousands of others, a cheap echo of the legacy, the history, and the art of those vanished masons.

Simply put, good restoration must duplicate the original work. Whether in wood, brick, or stone, the same care and skill are required in the repairing as were in the beginning. This in turn requires a commitment from those who are willing to learn the skills. In the summer of 2003, I gave my then new apprentice Willie Lehmann, a graduate archaeologist, a carbide-tipped chisel, a 3-pound hammer, and a 10-inch-thick, odd-shaped piece of sandstone to cut exactly 12 inches wide for a wall we were building. It was his first day on the job, and he'd never worked a stone in his life, but I started him on cutting stone. I showed him how to use light hammer blows on the chisel to trace a line across the top, down both sides, and across the bottom to connect the lines. I watched as he then retraced the lines, hitting harder each pass. The clink of steel on steel was steady and constant. Then there came that subtly deeper sound that means the stone has finally decided to yield. Two strokes later, the fine sandstone opened up to show its new face: even, smooth, velvety crystals catching light. Willie's grin was a mile wide. He ran his fingers over that surface, and another aspiring stonemason began his journey toward joining the brotherhood.

This basement restoration required removing the whitewash, breaking out a concrete slab, digging down for more headroom, then working a footing under the stone walls. This must be done carefully, a few feet at a time, to avoid caving in the walls. The crumbling mortar was then picked out and the stone repointed.

Structural Foundations

Much of the repair that stonework requires is due to poor foundation work. Except for the Romans, no one had concrete, so stones were laid in the ground, without footings. The best work in temples, cathedrals, and aqueducts was set deep on wide stones that distributed the weight. But most building was done on a base that would eventually settle and shift, causing the inevitable cracks to run up the walls. Gravity just doesn't tolerate heavy things stacked on an uneven base.

Today, structural engineers calculate such settling propensities in the skyscrapers they build. The total load is proportional to the expected degree of stability of the base. Frank Lloyd Wright was able to sink multiple, concrete-filled shafts into the soft soil of Tokyo on which to build the stone Imperial Hotel. This world-renowned, earthquake-proof structure was supported by distributing its great weight over all those in-ground piers. Wright likened his system to many pins pushed upright into cheese. When all the pinheads were gathered together, they could support a lot of weight.

Most stone restoration today requires less technical planning. With careful excavation and the use of concrete, we can stabilize structures as imposing as the Leaning Tower of Pisa. The same principle can be used with leaning chimneys, cracked walls, and settled corners of stone buildings.

Turnback Mill

I once knew an old and skilled millwright, one of that breed of master craftsman who were part mason, part blacksmith, and part woodworker. This man gave my then 80-year-old friend Bill Cameron a timeless axiom: "When you've a mistake to correct, you must go back to the place of the beginning," he told Bill.

Bill, my brother John, and I were restoring Turnback Mill in Missouri at the time. There was so little left of the structure in the 1970s that we rebuilt it almost from scratch. But we began, as he advised, at the place of the beginning: the foundation. Some of it was intact, dry-laid double-faced walls of copperhead-infested stone. Reading the various styles of work since its 1837 origins, we were able to discern what had likely been the original structure. Later additions, to accommodate the installation of a water turbine to replace the mill wheel, we did not restore.

We dug for and poured concrete footings to support piers for floor beams, walls to carry the steel main shaft, places the stone had settled. We reused some stone and brought in similar stone, and eventually rebuilt the wooden mill building atop it. The restored mill, on the National Register of Historic Places, has even started operating again; it's open for tours and demonstrations, and processes corn and grits.

RESTORING A FOUNDATION

JOHN BURNELL AND HIS CREW restored the rubble sandstone foundation of this circa-1825 New England–style farmhouse in Aurora, Ohio. The foundation had buckled from poor drainage, so the crew excavated the length of the front foundation and rebuilt it from the ground up.

▶ This wall has reached nearly half its final height. At its base, the wall was about 30 inches thick, tapering up to 20 inches at top. The crew used mortar with a high lime-to-cement ratio to match this type of construction.

◀ To support the structure and provide clear access to the wall for reconstruction, a colleague attached a truss held up by a steel beam and cribbing to the front frame of the house. The crew also built a canopy to keep rain at bay while the cellar was opened up.

▲ Topography and mud would not allow the crew to get machinery near the foundation, so resetting the ashlared foundation stones atop the rubble foundation had to be done the old way — using spud bars to walk stones along rails of scrap lumber, lever in place, and set to plumb.

◀ The project nears completion. Atop a new foundation, Burnell and his crew reset the original cut-stone stoop and steps that had fallen away many years before.

it's better to replace with similar stones than to spend time and labor on cleaning. Old lime-and-sand mortar comes off easily. It's a question of how authentic the restoration is to be and whether the expense of cleaning is worth it.

The hardest part of making your mortared repairs look right will be matching the mortar. You can have the old stuff analyzed, usually by a structural engineering or architectural organization or at a college. You can then duplicate the sand/lime/cement mix. But it won't look the same, because the old mortar will have discolored due to factors such as age, mold, tree sap, and weathering. I try to duplicate the sand texture, if not the color. Coarse sand results in a totally different surface from fine sand. Break up some of the old mortar to see what sand is in there, then try to find some like it. Most old work will have sand from the nearest creek or river sandbar, so go there.

You may experiment with mortar dyes. Masonry supply stores have these. I find that a little soot can help age the look of a mortar joint, or some dirt rubbed in before it's cured. But only natural aging will blend your work closely with the original.

Stabilizing Chimneys

When you're dealing with a taller structure, such as a two-story house or even a chimney, restoration gets harder. One of our specialties is working footings under standing stone structures, sometimes straightening them, sometimes having to jack them up. Usually building owners, after learning the cost of complete restoration, settle for stabilizing and repointing the stones. Of course it depends on how much restoration is needed, but again, the foundation/footing is often the cause of damage.

Let's look at chimneys. A common problem is leaning. It's rare that a chimney leans *toward* the house, but when it does, those tons of stone will be pushing the wall and roof into a parallelogram. We've corrected this by placing two or more 20-ton hydraulic jacks under the lintel stone of the fireplace opening, cushioned with a heavy timber with some foam insulation between. We drive steel wedges into the joints at either side of the fireplace opening as we apply pressure. If we're lucky, this will lean the chimney back to plumb. If not (if it has started to disintegrate), we've had to stabilize the chimney in a complicated process where we install a new flue tile and surround it with concrete embedded with reinforcing rod. We do this before we can get the whole thing to stay together for leveling. This is not a task for the amateur. If you have ever seen how quickly a chimney can fall, you will appreciate this admonition.

This chimney has settled and leaned away from the house. In addition to being tilted back plumb, it will need to be supported while a sectional footing is poured under it.

You can't really winch the chimney back straight from outside toward the house or it'll come apart. Once it's plumb, we point up the wedged cracks with mortar, sometimes leaving the wedges well inside. Then we point up whatever else has come loose or needs it for other reasons.

Fixing a Leaning Chimney

The more common situation is the chimney leaning away from the house. This is from settling, and it usually occurs out from under the shelter of the roof, so the chimney leans away as the damp soil compacts. If mortar has been pushed in between the leaning chimney and the house wall over the years, we chip that out first, before any "plumbing" efforts.

A short-term solution is to drive steel wedges between stones near the base of the chimney while applying pressure against the outside farther up the structure. We used to do just this, if requested. The reasoning was that the ground was already compacted by that leaning chimney, and that once plumb a lot of the pressure from the leaning would be relieved.

We do this "plumbing" by using two long beams, of steel or strong wood, set against overhanging stones if present. Or we chip out pockets up there if there is no existing ledge to push against. Usually we're

REPAIRING THE INSIDE OF A CHIMNEY

INSIDES OF CHIMNEYS are a pain. We've installed clay flue liners, stainless-steel liners, and even considered letting a small crew member down inside to plaster up gaps. Understandably, that was not a sought-after assignment. It is always advisable to line an old chimney for use, for one very good reason and another pretty good one.

The best reason to add a chimney liner is that mortar or stones that fall out leave gaps, sometimes clear through to the wood of the structure. With periods of disuse, mice and birds love to build nests in these cavities, sheltered and safe from most predators. So the next time a fire is built, the combustibles will ignite, and the house can burn down.

The other reason for a flue liner (besides the building code requirement) is that it makes the chimney much easier to clean. Soot and creosote build up inside any chimney or stovepipe, and overheating will cause huge and destructive combustion sooner or later if a chimney

is not cleaned. I recall a brick chimney near our home that exploded from a flue fire. Bricks went like missiles 100 feet or more. Examination of the fragments showed a buildup of flammable deposits like black caramel inside.

Airtight woodstoves are the worst offenders here, since the minimal oxygen when they're closed won't let the wood burn completely. A lot of stuff gets only partway up the chimney, to coat the inside surfaces. A free-breathing fireplace will burn cleaner, but if used much (20 to 30 times a winter), the chimney should be cleaned yearly. You'll get an idea of how much buildup is in there by the quantity the chimney sweep collects.

Some people get paranoid about chimneys and have them cleaned even if very little soot and creosote are in there. The sweep will just about always clean it if you insist, because it's hard to tell from looking how much crud is inside. Avoid buildup and huge bonfires, and you'll usually avoid a flue fire.

pushing at about 15 feet up the chimney, positioning the push apparatus on the ground about 10 feet out from the chimney.

The apparatus consists of setting 20-ton jacks against 2×½ boards dug into the ground at just the right angle to boost these beams upward. Then we apply pressure as we drive in the wedges, and eventually the chimney cracks as it leans back into plumb. It's a lot like wedging over a large tree you're cutting.

If the chimney hasn't moved much, and if core drilling shows rock or a footing under it, sometimes you can do just this much: fill the crack you've opened with mortar, leaving the wedges in or driving more in that won't stick out.

I don't recommend this, and don't do it anymore. The footing, if any, has had to settle for the chimney to move, and it should be stabilized. What is necessary is a good, broad footing under there, deep and substantial to stay in place. But of course you can't just dig under a chimney and expect it to hover there while you pour a footing.

What we do is common sense, as is most stonework. We leave the pressure on the chimney from the jacks and beams and we excavate relatively small areas, maybe 24 inches each, around the chimney base, one at a time. We go as far down as necessary to get 1 foot of depth below the stone and at least 1 foot under it and outside it. Then we wire-brush all the dirt off the bottoms of the stones. (All of this is always done by hand, since a backhoe's hydraulic power could topple the chimney in a moment of lapsed attention at the controls.)

Next, we drive 4-foot lengths of #4 or #5 rebar into the sides of the hole. It's best to bend a little curve into the bar first, so it will go into the dirt at the sides more or less horizontally. When we have driven in 1 or 2 feet, two bars to each side of the hole, we bend what's left down and across and under the chimney base. This will be the reinforcing for the concrete footing section we're about to pour. We mix one part Portland cement, two parts sand, and three parts gravel with enough water for a stiff mix and shovel it into the hole. We work the air pockets out of this concrete and fill the hole until it's up tight to the bottom chimney stone.

After that, we go away for at least two days, while the concrete sets up. We can then dig out an adjoining section and uncover the rebar that's already there, extended from the concrete. We wire-brush this clean, to ensure as good a bond as possible with it and the fresh concrete. We repeat the process until we've underlaid the periphery of the chimney with a footing/foundation. When it's all cured properly, including the fill mortar around the wedges, we remove the jacks and beams.

One house we worked on, the old Theodore Roosevelt hunting cabin in central Virginia, had two slate chimneys at each end leaning away from the cabin. A previous attempt to solve the problem was to install two 40-foot steel rods extending through the loft. The rods were threaded to bolted bars across leaning chimneys at both gable ends. There was a lot of tension on those rods. (One of my crew, who played the guitar, thumped them and announced one rod was a G and the other a D.) We used the multistage technique to stabilize them, leaving the rods in place until we had both chimneys straightened.

The alternative would have been to dismantle both chimneys, install footings, then rebuild them. Since there were a total of four fireplaces, this would have been quite expensive. Besides, the soft slate the builder had used would have disintegrated, and at best we would have had to replace most of the stone.

Straightening Cracked Walls

We used a technique similar to our chimney-straightening method on a historic stone house near Charlestown, West Virginia, in 2004. One corner of the 1½-story house had settled, cracking above a door the short distance

The settled and cracked walls of this circa-1737 stone house in Charlestown, West Virginia, were in desperate need of repair. There was no footing under the walls, so the crew dug one in sections and poured concrete to stabilize the house while massive hydraulic jacks held up the building. After the foundation was stabilized, the joints were repointed.

to a window opening. Another crack went from a basement window up to the main-floor window above it. Both cracks extended on up.

Here, we were able to do two widely separated sections of footing at once, supporting the corner of the house with jacks and steel. Surprisingly, this otherwise well-constructed house was not even built on wide stones in the ground. The builder had dug down about a foot and then started laying stone with lime-and-sand mortar, right in the ditches. The house had stayed stable for about 250 years, except in this vulnerable corner.

Pointing-up

Much stone restoration work today consists only of picking out old mortar — with a narrow chisel, pointing tool, or even an old screwdriver — and repointing, which is just pushing in new mortar. Sometimes this is all the old structures need. But if there are cracks that have resulted from settling, just pointing up won't correct the problem. It will seal the cracks, and the job will look good for a while but unless some serious supporting is done where cracks and settling extend to the ground, the movement will continue. Again, one must go back to the place of the beginning.

Most pointing-up is necessary only where the soft lime mortar has eroded, allowing leaks and even stones to fall out. It's good to do at least a simple analysis of the old mortar and duplicate it as well as you can. We typically use masonry mortar mix one-to-one with more lime, one part of this to three parts sand. This gets us a mostly lime repair mix for old work. If it's more recent, and shows the use of Portland cement, we use our standard mix of one part lime, two parts Portland, and nine parts sand. Or we vary either mix a little, with more or less lime, to get as close as we can to the original.

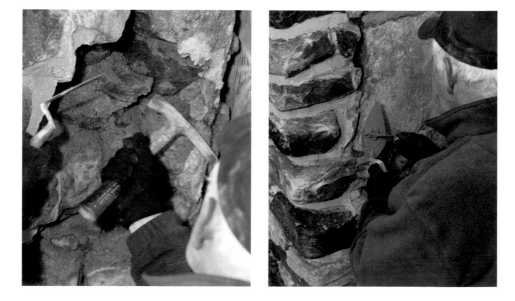

Pointing-up requires removing old mortar and sometimes stones. The new mortar is pushed in with the pointing tool.

Pointing-up obviously does not use as much mortar as the original bed of mortar, and so this narrow strand of mortar must be protected better than usual mortar work. When pointing up, dig 2 inches or more back into the joints, wet the stone with a spray bottle of water, and use the pointer to push in the new mortar carefully. Do not let the mortar run onto the stone faces; you'll never get the face really clean. Keep the mortar recessed. Then keep the work damp for two days, spraying every two hours or so, or the moisture will be drawn out of it by the surrounding dry stones and it'll be weak. Some masons like to drape wet layers of burlap over and against pointing-up, and even new work, to keep it moist.

One almost universal need for repointing is to correct the sloppy habit amateur masons had of smearing mortar onto the stone faces during a previous repair attempt. Chip and wire-brush this off as best you can before repointing. If the lime stains won't clean off, you may use a 1-to-10 dilution of muriatic acid and water to remove them. Wash thoroughly afterward, and let the stone dry partially before pointing with new mortar. Be aware that any lichens on the stones will be killed by the acid.

Chimneys are entirely too easy to take down. This plastered chimney of solid stone had to be pulled down and rebuilt because a stovepipe had been inserted and concrete poured in around it, restricting air flow.

Expect the Unexpected

When attempting restoration stonework, it's important to remember that not all old walls are constructed using the best techniques. For instance, a common practice among early builders in the eastern United States was to lay up house, barn, or storage building walls and chimneys with clay or even just side-yard mud. Only the outside of the joints were pointed-up, to keep rain from eroding the fill. Eventually the soft mortar eroded anyway, and out came the fill.

As long as clay fill is back deep and stays dry, it's fine to leave it. Just make sure you do seal it with good, tight pointing-up allowed to cure properly. With chimneys, this also means a solid mortared cap around the flue opening on top, sloped out to drain water away.

Often, early masons in this country used odd-shaped stones and did a lot of filling with whatever mortar they used. This followed the European tradition of building solid, squared corners, header over stretcher, often finely cut, then filling walls between with rubble plastered in place. Door and window edges were also carefully done, but the long stretches of heavily mortared wall were subject to weathering. Sometimes the entire exterior was then plastered, but this had to be redone often. Eventually, weather wore away this covering anyway, or modern owners, eager to expose the original stonework, sandblasted the plaster off. If the original masons had done a tight job, this would be okay, but a lot of them didn't. A whole lot of early builders weren't good masons, and/or their stone was bad stuff. You often can uncover big joints, shards and odd chunks of unshaped stones that are barely staying in place.

Working a little at a time, you can open up wide joints, pack in fresh mortar, and push in chips or small stones to minimize all that space. Use deep pieces so they'll stay in place, and try to find or shape rocks that have some semblance in shape to their respective spaces. Whenever possible, use pieces with flat faces, so they'll look like they were intentionally placed. You'll actually strengthen the wall, because mortar is the weak link, and you will have minimized those ugly expanses.

Sad Cases

A lot of stonework just isn't worth restoring. Some pretty awful work is out there, such as walls that are more mortar than stone, those with mortar and stains smeared across the stone faces, and those with stones that are odd-shaped and ugly. Sometimes the stones originally used were so bad that restoration is neither practical nor desirable. This is where we suggest complete replacement.

Complete replacement is quite often called for with a bulging and cracked, leaning retaining wall. For restoration, it's necessary to tear out, dig out behind, and rebuild the wall. It may well need a footing, too. If it's a mortared wall, it also will need weep holes at the bottom to let out water from behind the wall. The fill should have at the very least a foot of #5 to #8 gravel at the bottom, covered with filter fabric to keep it clear so water can percolate down. It's better to fill all the way up to topsoil with gravel.

A drystack retaining wall can be restored as we said earlier, without weep holes, because the water can come right through the stones. With a mortared wall, excessive water buildup behind it soaks and destabilizes the soil, making the wall have to work harder to hold it.

A common cause of failure in retaining walls is too much traffic above them. A road too close is the worst because of the pounding that vehicles give the ground. Here, a wall should probably be of reinforced concrete with buttresses. A stone wall can always be built as veneer against this for appearance.

Work Carefully

Restoration work can be dangerous. A pulled-over chimney needing to be rebuilt can send stones flying, for instance. We dismantled a stone house west of Carlyle, Pennsylvania, in late winter in a high wind. The material from the two-story-plus basement-and-loft stone house was to be stored for future reassembly. High up on stone gable walls and in the two massive chimneys were loose stones with the mortar completely gone. I had the very real fear that those rocks could be blown off or shaken onto us. Some looked like they were teetering already.

I got the crew to stay back and keep other people away, then climbed up with crew member John Whitekettle, who was also an underwater salvage diver. He wasn't afraid of much, and we stood on the peak of that roof and hurled stones off until we got down to stable work. The wind was so strong that each stone, up to maybe 75 pounds, was blown off course in its four-story drop.

A RESTORATION STORY

A FEW YEARS AGO, I did a consultation with a couple from New York who'd bought an early-1800s stone house upstate. It was on a nice creek and had at one time been the local miller's house. No trace of the mill remained, but the house was said to have been built by an immigrant Scottish stonemason. Three other houses in the area he'd built had been restored, and we visited them. All had the same distinctive dark red cut sandstone at the corners and at windows and doorways. The stones between these were the dark gray rubble of the area, well laid but uncut and fitted with a lot of lime mortar fill.

Unfortunately, this house, situated so near the creek bank, had settled badly at one corner, with wide cracking. The wife, architect Robin Andrade, was especially keen to restore this unique house. My examination showed that it would be one of those projects very nearly not worth the investment in time, labor, and materials unless the owners could do much of the work themselves and hire only the necessary craftsmen. Of course, that is always entirely a subjective choice, and a lot of worthy restoration

wouldn't happen if those were the only considerations. At last word, Robin's husband, opera singer Anthony Sadakis, had removed much of the wide-board paneling himself and had the house nearly prepared for stone restoration. Anthony and I discussed a trade — his teaching me musical timing for my consultation fee — but the timing for that never worked out, either.

This story has a related one. The next year, my daughter, Amanda, then still in college, wrangled plane tickets to Scotland and took me on a long-deferred trip to the land of our McRaven/McDonnell ancestors. Among many other structures, we saw that the corner stones in the ruined Invergarry Castle on the Rock of the Raven were of dark red sandstone. The stone between was dark, uncoursed rubble set with lime mortar fill. The work was almost identical to that in the upstate New York stone house. Legend has it that clansmen quarried the red stone seven miles distant, and that each was passed, hand to hand, along a line of them all the way to the castle. Given the size of some of those squared blocks of stone, that would have been quite a feat.

ABOVE: John Burnell restored this circa-1853 cobblestone house in Aurora, Ohio.

OPPOSITE LEFT: This dry-stone garden retaining wall features a granite foundation with upper courses of sandstone.

OPPOSITE RIGHT: For the restoration of this dry-laid sandstone wall at the Stan Hywet Hall and Gardens in Akron, Ohio, John and his crew had to duplicate the curvilinear coursing and tooling of original circa-1915 wall.

An anonymous mason built a wall in Akron, Ohio, in 1840. About 150 years later, John Burnell — an Ohio-based mason who specializes in historic restoration — encountered it, and found that it had an artfulness to it that deeply inspired him. "I've been exploring traditional stonework up to now, and mostly I try to blend my work with something old," John says. He relished an opportunity to build a retaining wall that allowed him to "get a little artful," however. With that project, he started to develop, he says, "what might be called my style."

John works almost exclusively with local stone ("we have a great quarry nearby; it's simple to get"), which in northeast Ohio means sandstone and a vibrant variety of granite; for this retaining wall, John incorporated both. His description of the glacial history of the region that resulted in the colorful striations in the granite recalls a quote by the artist Andy Goldsworthy, whose work John dearly loves: "Stones are objects for contemplation: the more you look, the more you become aware of the journey each stone has made." The base of John's wall was made of that granite, whose rounded forms and deep color stand out as they blend into the more square-shaped and lighter-hued sandstone. The effect is of a seamless merger from ground to ground cover to stone, "like the wall is growing out of the earth," as John puts it, a unique organic look,

the granite reminiscent of roots. "Structurally, it's built the way it should be," he says. (John jokes that even if your first attempt at building a drystone wall ends up succumbing to gravity's pull, "ruins are still beautiful — you can't lose!")

John was a home maintenance contractor who, on a driving trip through New England, was stirred to learn the traditional stone-laying craft. He sought teachers for a year or two, but they were few and far between in his neck of the woods, so he headed down to Kentucky to take a short workshop at the Dry Stone Conservancy (see page 80) and got hooked. "The bluegrass area is paradise for stonemasons," he says. He praises the conservancy for "creating a generation of masons" who, like himself, went on to run their own businesses.

Stones are objects for contemplation.

"I work with rubble, not a lot of carving or cutting," explains John. Having said that, he has a great affection for his collection of tools: "I picked up half of my stone hammers at flea markets," he says. They're 19th-century antiques, and he relishes what he describes as their "wonderful steel." Shockingly, some of them were stolen from him in the previous year, and it still pains him. "They were irreplaceable," he says.

"It's humbling to work with stone. That's the key to it: it's a privilege," John says, almost shyly. The resurgence of interest in the craft of masonry may take a couple of generations to develop, he says, "but the more I'm into it, in my world I don't feel so much alone."

To see more of John Burnell's work, turn to page 247.

BY NOW, YOU SHOULD HAVE A FAIRLY broad overview of the art and the craft of stonework. You may have already formed some conclusions about the craft, too. You may feel as my father and one brother did after we built a stone house in 1948; neither ever wanted to lay another rock. I've had apprentices quit after one day, too. One quit after half a day.

If you choose to pursue the craft of stonework, you essentially have two options: learn on your own, as I did, with all the attendant pitfalls and ugly early work; or learn from others, with proportionately fewer pitfalls and less ugly early work.

Learning about stonework from an experienced mason is the best way to avoid many of the pitfalls, mistakes, and just plain ugly stonework that come with the territory.

An apprenticeship is still the best way to go, unless you're the kind who won't listen and take direction. In that case, get yourself elected president of something instead.

The Learning Curve

On average, a new apprentice can do fairly well after two years, depending on his or her learning curve. In that time mason and apprentice may handle 200 tons of stone or only 50. Each stone gets handled several times. If there is a lot of repetition in the jobs within that time, new masons don't get wide experience, but they get some thorough experience. It doesn't make you a competent mason to have helped on just one fireplace/chimney, or a few feet of flagstone, or part of a retaining wall.

Irish stonemason Patrick McAfee said that after three years of learning, he began to see how far he had to go. After 58 years at it, I do too. Of course, I didn't work all day, every day at stonework. There must have been some other things in there as well. But I've come to love it more as time passes.

A rudimentary skill can be built with some basic guidance. Stone workshops of a week's duration include the barest beginnings. I tell participants that what they've learned, plus 30 years' practice, may make masons of them. We try to cover the basics of stone selection, shaping, dry and mortared walls, flat work, and maybe simple outdoor stone steps.

Whether you plan to pursue stonework as a hobby, as something to do around your place only, or as a possible livelihood, learn it well. That early work will come back to haunt you; it's so *permanent*. As my old photographer friend the late Townsend

Godsey once said: "The difference between a good photographer and a bad one is the good one doesn't show his bad work." Unfortunately, folks *will* see your bad stonework for a long time. It's best to go slowly and carefully for this reason. Look at the work of others and compare. Aim high, even if it takes you a long time. One stone in the right place done right is worth a lot of wrong ones. So you get only 5 square feet in a day instead of 20. You'll eventually get faster; just don't sacrifice quality for speed. Those stones are accustomed to waiting.

Now, what you think looks right may be the ugliest work another person has ever seen. There's room for subjectivity here, but don't push it. Build whatever you're happy with at home, as long as it doesn't cause a domestic dispute. But if you're going to work for others, they get to say a lot about what your work should look like — at least until you get famous and eccentric.

Hiring a Stonemason

Rather than work with the stone yourself, you may choose to hire a mason. Have a clear picture of the type of work you want at your place. Since our children worked with me while they were growing up, they've all become stonemasonry snobs. "Look at those running joints!" one of my daughters will exclaim on a trip somewhere. Or, "That guy didn't rake his joints!" Or, "Look there; you can see where one mason quit and another took over." It makes me proud.

So how do you go about finding the mason who can translate your imagination into reality? How do you find someone who can build what you want, even help you decide, with ideas of his or her own that fit? And are there masons whose work won't cost you so much that it'll be out of the question for your circumstances?

It's a lot like finding a good mechanic, or a good contractor to build your house or put in that addition you've wanted. A mason is no easier to locate than any other craftsperson, for the same reasons. You want someone who will have your interests as a top priority, who will respect what you're working toward in your landscaping, fireplace/chimney, patio, water features — whatever. You need someone you can communicate with and who won't go off on some preconceived track and ignore you.

You should plan to go see other work your prospective stonemason has done. Talk with the people he or she worked for, and ask how well they got along. A fine mason can be a real grouch, while a smooth, personable talker can leave you with shoddy work. Now, personalities being what they are, you won't always get along with anyone just as another person might. It's no less so with masons. Sometimes a client clicks with one, while his next-door neighbor can't stand to be around him. Hey, that's life.

Consider this: The person you contract with will do work on your property that will be permanent. It has to be what you want, only partly because it will cost you so much. You can't humor an artist's need to make his own statement at your expense. He leaves after the job is done; you have to live with it. If the work doesn't meet your needs or is a style you don't like, you still have to live with it.

So go into the search armed with enough information to know what you want, and some fairly specific parameters. You have to know enough to make informed decisions where they count, and be prepared to stand your ground, within reason, against outrageous or inadequate proposals. You want to be educated enough to know the difference.

Finding a Mason

Because most masons are pretty independent, solitary, ornery types, they don't often belong to official associations and organizations. The Stone Foundation (see Resources, page 265) has a handy directory of masons by state. Asking local landscapers and architects for recommendations is also a good idea; they're often required to work hand in hand with masons.

Prices and Contracts

Know how much a mason should charge, in your area at the time you have work done. Stonemasonry is free enterprise; the mason can charge whatever he or she thinks the work will be worth. I know some masons who charge some clients more because they see a lot of money has been spent there. I've never done this, but I will admit to charging less for folks I knew were in tough financial situations.

Don't get caught in a per-hour contract, because you can't know how fast the mason will be. You should be more concerned with the quality of the work, but if his pace is glacial, it'll cost you too much to pay an hourly wage. Square face-foot prices are better because they protect the mason and still give you the flexibility and parameters to make changes. Getting a flat price for complete jobs should, in theory, work better than it does.

Be sure you know up front just what you're buying. Some masons prefer to charge for just their labor and expect you to pay for the stone, sand, cement, footing materials, and excavation. Others give you a complete package that includes materials. I've discussed the issue of using the stone on the owner's property, and here's where you'll have to trust the mason. The tons of stone that are all over your place may not be usable *at all*. Or, more likely, some of it may be usable only at the expense of a lot of time/labor, with shaping and adapting. Remember, the labor is the *big* item, not the cost of the stone.

If you do agree to provide the stone, check closely with the prospective mason to make sure you're getting what the mason asks for and can

work with. Pallets of bad, cheap stone serve no one well. And does that stoneyard cost include delivery? How about unloading at your site? Unloading can be a very complex and expensive item that I assert is the responsibility of the client. Why? Because the client wants his site protected, and that imposes limits, either by request or by the nature of the site. Is there room for a big truck to bring a big load? Or will you have to arrange for the stone to be brought a little at a time? And if it has to be dumped some distance from the job itself, who pays for moving it again? Do not imagine that these details are without cost to you or without hassle for the mason. You and the mason should agree on details like this before the job starts, or you'll get some surprises. It never ceases to amaze me how two people can see the same situation from such opposite viewpoints. And when it comes to your hard-earned dollars, these differences can become major.

Relating to Your Mason

I'm always delighted when an old client wants me back to do other projects. That's the best recommendation a mason can have. If what he or she created before is still considered fine work years later, enough that the client wants more, everyone's happy. But if the mason is called back to fix something that wasn't right in the first place, that's trouble. As the owner, you are expected to monitor the job, and if you see something you don't like, get it straight with the mason right then.

Tearing out work is difficult and often considered insulting. It makes for a rough relationship if you've let the problem go on before acting. It's entirely possible that the mason thought he or she was doing exactly what you wanted with that chunk of shiny quartz in your sandstone wall or the fresh-cut, bright face on the one stone in a structure of aged granite with lichens. Masons get tunnel vision sometimes, like sign painters who leave out letters. I always like to stand back a lot and see how the whole is coming together, and so do most masons. But if one gets in a hurry so he can finish that day in time for his kid's soccer game, he might do something sloppy. Catch it right away. Letting it go reminds me of an old mason's term for gaps in the mortar joints: "bee holes." Leave them and they'll *be* there. Forever.

All but the most self-glorified stonemasons will welcome your input and appreciate your imaginative projects, unless they're totally off the wall. I'm always struck by other stone workers' willingness to work with anyone, as long as he or she respects the stone and the craft. Just don't hover too much; it makes folks nervous. I once did work for an older lady who brought a folding chair out to the job and sat there watching every move I made. Eventually I was able to tune her out, but it took effort. She wasn't overly critical; maybe she was just extremely interested. But she was a constant, lurking presence, and I always expected her to pounce on some wrong move I'd made. I do know I didn't get as much work done each day with her there.

All in all, the search for a stonemason will have its aspects of adventure. The better informed and prepared you are for creating permanent stone features around your home, the less traumatic it will be. You'll have dirt piled around, mud tracked all over, things trampled, and unfamiliar people around; just expect it. Having thought it out ahead of time, you can have the dirt moved somewhere you want it. You can have mulch and straw spread to contain the mud. You can designate paths the masons are to take. You can help lessen the chaos.

Both you and your stonemason will appreciate your efforts.

Masons Patrick Patterson and Jim Moniz are at work with West Virginia sandstone. (See page 15 for the finished wall.) There is no such thing as a confined, neat, tidy workspace when stonemasonry is concerned. The stone needs to be spread out to give the mason a clear view of the supply, so that he or she can choose the right rock for the right spot. Cleanup comes at the end of the job.

GLOSSARY

aggregate   Substance made up of different-sized particles, such as sand and gravel.

anchor bolt   A bolt set into masonry to anchor wooden or metal construction members.

annealed   Softened metal, to avoid breakage.

aqueduct   Man-made watercourse, often raised.

ashlar   Stone cut in regular straight-line patterns.

bond   Pattern of laying masonry to tie together more than one thickness.

boom   Extended beam for lifting.

breezeway   Open passage through house or barn.

buttress   Short bracing portion of a wall, at right angles to it.

calcium chloride   Chemical that when added to mortar retards freezing.

cantilever   Portion of a structure extending horizontally, unsupported.

capstone   A stone along the top of a wall.

cement   Chemically bonding substance mixed with sand and/or gravel for mortar or concrete.

chert   A limestone, often containing flint deposits.

chimney cap   Cover to keep out rain, birds, and leaves.

"come-along"   Ratchet cable or chain hoist.

concrete   Mixture of cement, sand, gravel, and water to form a solid material.

curing   In mortar or concrete, keeping wet until the chemical action is complete.

damper   Device for restricting passage of air or smoke up a chimney.

drystone   Construction of stone with no mortar.

dry wall   Plasterboard wall covering.

face rocks   Those covering the face of a wall, as in veneer.

facing   Door or window framing.

fieldstone   Stone found on top of the ground used in its naturally occurring shapes.

fill   Loose earth placed in a depression to achieve height.

firebox   A usually metal enclosure for containing fire and radiating heat.

firebrick   A heat-resistant brick for use next to fire.

flagstone   Thin stone used as a floor or walkway.

flashing   Thin metal sheeting used to seal joints in buildings against rain.

flat keystone span   A self-supporting horizontal span formed of shaped stones.

flue   Enclosed vertical passage for smoke.

flue tile   Ceramic lining used in chimneys.

footing   Base for a structure or wall foundation.

forms   Temporary shaping structures for pouring concrete.

gin poles   Pair of beams forming an A-shape for lifting.

green mortar   That which is hard but not cured.

grid   Crisscross pattern forming squares, as of reinforcing rods.

header   Stone or brick laid with its short end outward.

hillside cut   A bank resulting from vertical digging.

keystone   That stone in a span which locks the others in place.

keystone span   Structure bridging an opening, held with a keystone.

knee wall   Low upstairs vertical wall under a roof slope.

ledge pattern   Flat stones laid horizontally in a structure.

lintel   A single stone spanning an opening.

masonry cement   Cement and lime mix, for bonding stonework.

masonry sealer   Varnishlike substance for sealing masonry against water.

mason's hammer   One with a chisel-like extension for shaping stones.

mortar   Bonding substance of cement, sand, and water.

mortared construction   Masonry bonded with mortar, as opposed to dry-stone work.

multiple keystone   A type of span utilizing several shaped stones to distribute the wedging function of the keystone.

muriatic acid   Commercial hydrochloric acid, used diluted to clean stonework.

pitching tool   Stone chisel with one surface flat and the opposite beveled, for removing protrusions.

plumb bob   Pointed weight on a string for maintaining vertical level.

pointing up   In masonry, filling cracks between stones or bricks with mortar.

Portland cement   Unmixed cement used in concrete, originally from Portland, England.

quarry   Natural deposit of stone from which stone is cut and removed.

reinforced concrete   That having steel rods or mesh inside for strength.

reinforcing rod   Steel rod for strengthening concrete.

riser   The vertical face of a step.

rubble   Stonework consisting of stones of all sizes and shapes with no effort made at any pattern; also, broken waste stone.

sap   Moisture in newly quarried stone.

scaffold   Temporary structure for working high areas of a wall.

screed   Board for leveling newly poured concrete, as for a floor.

setting up   The hardening of concrete or mortar.

shoulder stones   In a chimney, those at the point of the chimney's narrowing.